The Tree of All Hearts

Modern Parables for Teaching Faith

Israel
GALINDO

Alexander O.
GONZALEZ

SMYTH & HELWYS
PUBLISHING, INCORPORATED · MACON, GEORGIA

Smyth & Helwys Publishing, Inc.
6316 Peake Road
Macon, Georgia 31210-3960
1-800-747-3016

Library of Congress Cataloging-in-Publication Data

Galindo, Israel.
    The tree of all hearts : modern parables for teaching faith / Israel
    Galindo and Alexander O. Gonzalez.
    p. cm.
    Includes index.
    1. Christian life.
    2. Parables.
    I. Gonzalez, Alexander O.
    II. Title.
    BV4515.3 .G35 2001
    242—dc21   2001018382
                                                               CIP

ISBN 978-1-57312-298-6

Contents

Preface

"Once upon a time . . ." Our ears perk up whenever we hear those familiar words. They signal that we're in for something exciting, and our imaginations are taken captive every time we hear them. Stories have the power to open minds and hearts, to ignite the imagination, to create worlds and transform persons. Stories can reveal mysteries, teach morals, illustrate profound truths, and inspire even the unmotivated to action. It is no wonder, then, that the story is one of the most powerful teaching methods the Christian teacher or preacher can use.

Stories are essential for describing the Christian experience. As a matter of fact, the good news of Christ has been called "The Greatest Story Ever Told." Jesus used stories to describe masterfully what our relationship to God could be. Customarily, Jesus used vivid imagery drawn from the everyday lives of his listeners. Until the time of the printed text—and the Reformation shortly after—symbols, images (e.g., stained glass windows, icons, sculpted relief, and art), and storytelling were the main means of communicating the Gospels.

Jesus was called "Teacher" (Rabbi), "Master," "Savior," and "Christ." Those titles of respect were important to his contemporaries—and all certainly true. But perhaps his listeners best knew Jesus as a master storyteller. This becomes evident when we realize that the most-quoted words of Jesus come from the stories he told. As a storyteller, Jesus' favorite genre was the parable.

The parable is one of the most effective ways of communicating spiritual truths. It is no surprise, therefore, that Jesus used parables as a primary means for conveying his radical message of love and grace. The power of parables and stories lies in their ability to address matters of the heart in ways akin to poetry. They are able to make the connection between brain and heart, mind and soul. As an aid to preaching and teaching, parables provide powerful windows to truths that can be grasped by the hearer on many levels.

The parables and stories in this book address common themes of the Christian life: faith and fear, discipleship and discipline, death and life, salvation and hope. Some are parables in the strict sense of the term; others are fantasy, fables, and genre stories. Like any good story, each will speak to the listeners at whatever level of readiness and understanding they bring to the story. So, usually, one should let the story "speak for itself." For those who would like to use the stories either for personal or group study, each story includes corresponding Bible passages and a list of study questions for pondering various aspects of the story.

So let's begin: "Once upon a time. . . ."

For Barbara and Myra

Red Paint

In a certain city there once lived a man who was a very hard worker. His dearest goal in life was to buy and own a house. To realize his dream, he dedicated himself to work day and night. Eventually, through his hard work, he was able to put away and save some money—enough to buy his dream house, he thought.

With great excitement he started to look for that dream house. But he was greatly disillusioned to find that the beautiful houses that most appealed to him were still beyond his means. And worse, the houses he could afford were dilapidated "handyman specials" in need of much repair. He became very sad.

But just about the time he was ready to give up, he happened upon a vacant house on a corner with a sign that read, "For Sale." He fell in love with the house at first sight. It was a white house, spacious and grand. And its price was so low that it seemed they were giving it away. It was a real jewel, a dream house come true. According to the seller, it had only "one little defect." It seems that the interior walls were all black! Every wall of every room was painted black. That was the reason the house was so affordable. No one, it seems, wanted to buy a house that was white on the outside, but all black on the inside.

But the man, eager to own the house, gave no importance to the little defect. He thought to himself that he could easily fix the problem of the black walls. So he bought the house right then and there.

Unfortunately, he soon found out that he had been mistaken; those black walls were not easy to change. You see, what made them black was not paint; rather, the walls were covered with dark stains and spots so dirty that they indeed looked like black paint. And nothing would get rid of those stains. First he tried soap, but that didn't work. Then he tried a strong detergent, but that didn't remove the stains. Then someone suggested he use white paint to cover the walls; surely that would do it.

So the man painted the walls once, then twice, and eventually, ten times. But instead of making them better, the walls looked worse. The dirty walls absorbed the paint and looked gray and blotchy in some places, but just as black as ever in other spots. The walls actually looked dirtier than before!

The new homeowner became very disillusioned. He determined to sell the house back to the owners, but they wouldn't take it. He tried selling the house to others, but no one wanted to buy a house that was white and pretty on the outside, but whose inside walls looked so terrible. He couldn't tear down the house; he had nowhere else to live. But living in that house was impossible, because the walls made it so dark and depressing that he could not stand being in it.

You can imagine how the man felt. But in his most desperate hour he found the answer to his problem. In a nearby town there lived a person who had invented something truly amazing: a special red paint that removed all stains and paints and left walls white, clean, and sparkling. The man went in search of that amazing red paint.

When he found the place where he could buy the red paint, the man discovered that the price was exorbitant. But he made a decision. He sold all he had (except his house) and purchased the red paint.

When he returned home to his house with the black walls, he dipped his paintbrush into the red paint and applied it to the dirty, stained wall. Then the most amazing thing happened—the wall became clean, white, and shiny with a stroke of the brush. Every place he applied the red paint the stains disappeared, and the walls were left clean—with only one coat!

The man was overjoyed. Finally, the inside of his house was as white and beautiful as the outside. It was truly a place worthy to live in, and he did, happily.

Scripture Study

- Hebrews 9:14, 22
- 1 Peter 1:18, 19
- Revelation 1:5
- Isaiah 1:18

Study Questions

- This story is an allegory. Can you identify what some of the elements in the story represent?
- Have you ever tried to fix something, but the more you worked at fixing it the worse it got? Share that story.
- This story hints that there are some things within our power to do and some things that are beyond our ability to accomplish. Can you give some examples of these?
- Is there something you want to possess for which you would be willing to give everything you own? What is it?

The Special Glasses

There once lived a Christian by the name of Clarence, who had a grand imagination. In his church Clarence was affectionately known as "the inventor." This dreamer was very different from the other members of his church and considered a bit odd. For one thing, he always had a positive outlook on life.

One day at a church picnic Clarence ate more than he should have, or as some people say, "His eyes were bigger than his stomach." When he went to bed that night he fell into a deep sleep full of strange dreams. First, Clarence dreamed that he was a missionary in Syria and that Saddam Hussein was a member of his church. Later, he dreamed that an army of baked beans was chasing him.

But of all his dreams, one left a great impression on him. In this dream Clarence was a real inventor, and in his dream he had invented something very strange and wonderful. The invention was a special pair of x-ray glasses. As you can imagine, his invention revolutionized the field of medicine. Soon, Clarence's glasses replaced bulky x-ray and CAT scan machines, and before long a pair of his glasses could be found in every doctor's office. Imagine, a doctor had only to put on these fabulous glasses to examine any patient internally. With them a doctor could immediately examine broken bones, intestinal disorders, a beating heart, or a child in a mother's womb.

But the dream did not end there, because Clarence, being a great inventor, was not satisfied with a pair of x-ray glasses that let you examine the body only. After much tinkering, Clarence came up with a pair of glasses he called "FPI" (False Prophet Identifiers). These special glasses were designed to allow the wearer to identify and distinguish between the "sheep and the goats," that is, true Christians and false Christians.

The way the glasses worked was simple. A minister using these glasses could identify false a Christian by looking at the person's heart. If the heart looked white and clean, the person was a true Christian. But if the heart was dark, it meant that the person was not of Christ, but was instead a false prophet.

The impact this new invention had on the church was extraordinary. Church pews emptied dramatically as false Christians fled upon being uncovered. In some cases, ministers had to leave churches as they were discovered to be false prophets. All this resulted in a great revival in the churches. Freed from these evil influences, congregations grew in love and in faithfulness to the Word of God. Divisions evaporated, contentions ceased, and the sweet and real presence of Jesus was felt more and more.

At this point Clarence woke from his fantastic dream. He pondered the meaning of the recurring dream and somehow felt relieved to know that he had not invented those special glasses after all. But more than anything, Clarence was nagged by the question, if he had invented those glasses in real life, would that be a good thing or a bad thing?

Scripture Study

- Matthew 13:45
- Matthew 7:15-20
- 1 John 4:1-4
- 1 Samuel 16:7

Study Questions

- If you had a pair of x-ray glasses that could reveal the innermost secrets of persons in your church, would you use it? Why or why not?
- In the story Clarence's glasses had a positive effect in the church. Could special glasses like those Clarence invented have a negative effect? How?
- How well do you read people? Are your first impressions usually right or wrong?
- If you knew that your minister had a pair of Clarence's special glasses, how would you feel? Would you act differently? What would you do?

The Best Teacher

It was Monday morning at the Christian Academy of Our Redeemer. In the sixth grade class the following scene unfolded.

"Good morning class," said the teacher. The children stood at their desks and responded, "Good morning, teacher."

"Very well," continued the teacher. "The question of the day is this: 'Apart from Jesus, who is the greatest teacher?'"

All the children raised their hands, each eager to answer. Several answered that she was the best teacher.

"Well, I'll ask you another question," she said. "Apart from Jesus and me, who is the best teacher in the whole world?"

"The best teacher in the world is the mosquito," said Gabriel, a very capricious child.

"Why do you say that, Gabriel?" asked the teacher.

"Because the mosquito is very intelligent and knows how to live off of others," he replied.

"The best teacher is the parrot," cried Thomas. "The parrot knows a lot and talks a lot."

"That's not so!" exclaimed Isabel, a very bright student who was studious and well-disciplined. "The best teacher is the ant."

"How do you know that?" inquired the teacher with curiosity.

"The ant is very industrious and a hard and obedient worker," said Isabel. She added, "In addition, the ant teaches me the value of learning while I work, and this will help me succeed in my career."

One by one, each student gave his or her opinion as to who the greatest teacher might be. But in the corner of the classroom sat little Pauly, a timid and shy child, of whom the other students often made fun.

"And you, Pauly, who do you think is the best teacher?" prompted the teacher.

At that moment the world stopped spinning for Pauly. His tongue became dry, his heart palpitated with the force of a thousand galloping horses, and he would rather have been swallowed by the earth than to suffer the martyrdom of speaking up in the classroom.

But gathering his courage, he answered the teacher in a voice that was hardly audible, "The turtle."

"Can you repeat that a little louder, please?" asked the teacher.

"THE TURTLE!" yelled Pauly.

The class laughed at poor Pauly. Even the teacher could hardly keep from laughing. But the truth is that Pauly was right, and I'll tell you why.

In the first place, the turtle walks slowly. That is, he goes step by step in his lessons. He never hurries any of his students and repeats things as often as necessary.

The turtle has patience. This is something very necessary to being a great teacher. We see this in Jesus, who for three years taught his stubborn disciples and ignorant crowds with great patience and gentleness. And how many years has Jesus been working in our own lives? If he weren't a patient and loving teacher, we would not have lasted much longer than Ananias and Sapphira.

The greatest teacher also carries the burdens of his or her students. The turtle, with its large and hard shell, can carry great burdens. The best teacher is also a good friend. The mosquito lives off its friends, the parrot always wants to talk and be heard, and the ant works so hard that it is always too busy. It's not like that with the turtle, who walks slowly and often pauses to examine things, talk to others, and smell the flowers.

Patience, love, and friendship are only a few of the characteristics of a great teacher. If we add knowledge, talent, eloquence of speech, and humility, there is no doubt that such a teacher will excel.

Let us who would be great teachers follow the example of the turtle, especially those who would be teachers of the greatest subject—the Word of God.

Scripture Study

- James 3:1
- Ecclesiastes 10:12-13
- Matthew 10:24-25a
- Matthew 12:52

Study Questions

- Who was the greatest teacher you ever had? Why?
- Name some characteristics of a teacher in addition to those mentioned in the story.
- Is teaching a spiritual gift? Explain.
- Is teaching primarily a skill or a relationship? Explain.

The Elephant and the Kite

There once was a kite that was very boastful. This kite was very proud of his ability to fly high in the blue sky—higher than most other kites—and he wanted everyone to know it!

One day, while he was floating and flying very proudly high in the air, he saw a huge and ponderous elephant crossing a meadow far below. Immediately, the proud kite began to make fun of the creature.

"Hey, Fatso! Hurry up," cried the kite.

The elephant continued his plodding walk across the meadow, giving no attention to the insults and taunts from the colorful kite. But the kite would not be ignored.

"Hey, you! Elephant! Look how I can fly," taunted the boastful kite.

Once again the elephant remained unmoved by the taunt. But it wasn't because he couldn't hear the kite, for he had big ears and good hearing. Rather, the elephant didn't pay the kite any mind. You see, the elephant was pretty sure of himself. This was not the case with the kite. Held to the ground by a thin string and blown this way and that by the wind, at any moment the kite might break or be blown away. But that didn't stop the kite from his teasing.

"Why don't you come up here for a while?" he taunted, "Tell Dumbo to loan you his big ears so you can fly, too. Ha, ha!"

This time the elephant stopped for a moment, and lifting his head (as best an elephant can lift his head), looked at his little and insignificant tormentor. At first he looked on him with annoyance, but that quickly changed to compassion due to the Kite's skeletal complexion.

While he was thinking about how frail the boastful kite looked, he heard a gust of wind come from the north. The cold wind began to shake the pesky kite in a frenetic manner. The little kite's shouts of taunts quickly turned to shouts of fright at his desperate situation.

At first he flew up into the sky, and then he plummeted down like an airplane out of control, spinning around without direction. After one of his swoops he flew right into a tree and became trapped in its branches. When the children who owned the kite tried to rescue him, the string broke, and the kite was lost forever.

But the elephant remained on the ground, standing firm on his huge legs that resembled tree trunks. The same strong wind that proved fatal to the kite had no effect on him. You can believe that the wind did not even tickle him.

Scripture Study

- Ephesians 4:14
- Matthew 24:24
- Colossians 2:8
- Ephesians 6:11, 13-14

Study Questions

- Why is pride considered a sin? Shouldn't we have pride in our accomplishments and ourselves?
- Do the proud always get what they deserve?
- What are the characteristics of a "flighty" person? What are the characteristics of a "grounded" person?
- Often we seem to be attracted to persons like the boastful kite, tending to ignore the more grounded, mature persons like the elephant. Why?

The Religious Mosquito

This is the story of a very religious mosquito. Yes, you heard right, a mosquito! This shouldn't surprise anyone, since at one time or another we've run into these religious mosquitoes. In fact, at some time in our lives these small creatures have bitten most of us.

These tiny flying insects are very dangerous, their bites extremely painful. They also carry disease and contagious viruses. They fly from place to place spreading pain and poison.

Now, one night a particular mosquito went to church. And since it was a religious mosquito, the ushers let him in.

"Sit here, Brother," said an usher with love and courtesy.

"Bzzzzz. Thank you," replied the religious mosquito as he sat down.

The mosquito quickly settled down in the beautiful chapel. He loved everything about the place—the color of the walls, the red carpet, the soft curtains, the comfortable seats. In fact, he felt right at home in this environment.

The mosquito remained silent during the singing of the hymns, not because he did not enjoy the hymns, but because he just wasn't a very good singer. As the service progressed, it came time for the offering and later for the sermon. All this time the mosquito was very still, and he watched everything carefully, not because he was interested in the message of the hymns and the sermon, but because he was taking note of the defects in the pastor and of the shortcomings of the other worshipers.

When the service ended, the religious mosquito opened his wings and sharpened his stinger and started flying from one place to another, biting the defenseless and weak church members. They weren't equipped to defend themselves from such an attack, and so they suffered much hurt. Some of them got ill, but others actually sought out the mosquito to give him their blood to drink.

"Ah. I feel so good!" exclaimed the fat and satisfied mosquito.

This religious mosquito was a smart little insect. He avoided those church members who had a special repellent in their bodies. And he didn't have the audacity to go anywhere near a group of worshipers who knew the secret of healthy fumigation. They were immune to the mosquito's stings.

But his cleverness and evil availed him nothing, since on the following day he was dead. It is well known that the life of the mosquito is very short (thank goodness!) and that many of them perish under the hand of their stung victims—literally!

Scripture Study

- Matthew 16:1
- Mark 8:11
- Acts 20:28-31
- Jude 1-16

Study Questions

- Have you ever been stung by a religious mosquito? Share your experience.
- What kind of person is most susceptible to the sting of a religious mosquito?
- How can Christians in the church inoculate themselves from the stings of religious mosquitoes?
- What is the best way to handle a religious mosquito?

You Are Being Watched

In an industrial company located in the southeastern United States, a group of employees were engaged in an animated conversation. Each of them had abandoned their workstation to join in the conversation. One of them stood at a distance, looking down the hallway and acting as a sentinel, ready to sound the alarm at the first sign of "management." The heated conversation continued until the designated sentinel shouted, "He's coming!"

With a leap the group dispersed, each person trying to reach his designated workstation as quickly as possible. An eerie silence hung over the spot previously filled with whispers, talk, gossip, and groans. When the boss turned the corner, he saw only a scene as serene as a summer afternoon. Where seconds before confusion and chaos had brewed and bubbled, there now seemed only calm and order as each employee appeared intent on performing her assigned work.

But the boss was no fool. He knew that appearances can be deceiving—in the school of hard knocks he had learned that things aren't always what they seem. Some days later, unknown to his employees, he installed some closed-circuit security cameras throughout the building. Well hidden from sight, the cameras covered every part of the plant. From the monitoring station the boss could watch his employees at work and spot those who were not working. As he caught unfaithful and unproductive employees in the act of cheating or stealing time or supplies, he would call them into his office and deal with them harshly but fairly for their indiscretions. But the boss also rewarded those employees who worked diligently, who did their work above and beyond what was expected. He was, after all, a fair man.

Soon, word of the hidden surveillance cameras spread among the employees. Those who were good employees did not change much. In fact, they seemed not to take notice or worry about the cameras or care about being watched. They just went about their work as they had always done. But there was a noticeable change in the production level of the poorer employees.

Interestingly, while the level of production increased among the lazy employees, their level of satisfaction with the job dropped. But the boss seemed not to be too concerned about that, and he didn't try to make them happy about having to work harder. Instead, he gave his attention to the responsible workers who took pride in their work, never seeming to mind the cameras. In fact, for those good employees, the ever-watchful cameras were soon forgotten as they went about doing their work to the best of their abilities.

Scripture Study

- Proverbs 15:3
- Psalm 139:7-11
- Ephesians 4:30
- Hebrews 12:5-11

Study Questions

- What motivates most people to work hard and with integrity?
- This story hints that for the lazy employees, an increase in the quality of their work did not translate to increased satisfaction on their part. Why could that be?
- What motivates you best in your work? What kinds of things are not motivators for you?
- Are there some things that are appropriate motivators in the Christian life? Give examples. Are there some things that are inappropriate motivators in the Christian life? Give examples.

The Frogs and the Christians

It was a beautiful night, adorned with a canopy of stars without number. In the streets children ran and played, terrifying anxious mothers who witnessed their adventurous acts of daring.

On the outskirts of Jerusalem a soft sweet breeze blew and lulled to sleep the birds perching on the trees, the sheep in the fields, and the other animals that settled down after a long day for a good night's rest. Everything seemed calm and at peace, reminiscent of the night when the Christ child was born. The only sound was the quiet rustling of leaves in the breeze.

Soon, however, on a small lagoon on the lake opposite the shore of the Mount of Olives, another rustling sound was heard. It was the croaking of frogs, and the sound grew louder by the minute. Only in ancient Egypt had more frogs assembled in one place as on this night. They came from Bethlehem, Samaria, and northern Galilee.

"Have you heard about what happened to Judas?" asked an excitable little frog.

"Yes! And a well deserved fate, too," responded a fat brown and bumpy toad. "Such should be the fate of anyone who betrays Jesus."

At the sound of their beloved Lord's name, the frogs began to cry and croak as they remembered the death that was wrought by the disciple-turned-traitor. They could not fathom the reason why Jesus had chosen humans as disciples instead of the obedient sheep of the pasture, the swift messenger birds of the air, or even the proud frogs, keepers of the ponds. Humans were such treacherous creatures!

"We would never have betrayed him," croaked one old green frog, speaking what all the other frogs were thinking.

"And that's not all," said a frog from Capernaum. "Now I hear news from Antioch that there is trouble in the churches."

A hush fell among the frogs as they embraced their despair. It seemed the world had turned into a cold and empty place. Just then a lily pad floated to the center of the pond, bearing an impressive-looking bullfrog. It was the King of the Eastern Kingdom of frogs, a majestic and wise old frog.

"Hear me, all you frogs," he rumbled. "We are gathered tonight to clear up some doubts concerning the human Christians. It is certain that there are many of them who are fine men and women, but there are others of them who do things that not even swamp frogs would do.

"There are fights, quarrels, divisions, discrimination, and gossip among many who claim to know Jesus, and yet we who never knew him do not practice such detestable things. Even we, who do not hope for a heavenly pond and are content to live happily in the earthly ponds and with the flies God provides for us, do not disobey the Creator. It is a strange and sad situation."

"If only I could talk to the humans," cried a young frog.

"It would do no good," said the King of the Eastern Kingdom. "Don't you know that they already possess a book through which God speaks to them? The problem is that, as I hear it told, many of them do not even open the book to read the message. And many still do not enter the houses of God to listen to the words of life the Creator left."

"They should suffer the same fate as that Judas fellow," grumbled an old frog.

"I can understand your feeling that way," replied the King, "but these humans seem to have a special place in God's heart. They are blessed by God's unending patience and forgiveness toward them, even in their sin. From the time we all lost our homes in the beautiful Garden of Eden because of the human Adam, God has seemed determined to forgive and restore humans. It is most strange."

The sounds of croaking were heard all through the night as the assembly of frogs continued to ponder the fate of humans and the mystery of God's patience toward them. Only with the light of dawn did the sleepy frogs cease their noisy discussions and debate, leaving many unanswered questions—which would be taken up on another night, in another pond, in another time.

Scripture Study

- John 13:2-30
- Acts 1:18
- 1 Corinthians 1:10, 17; 3:1-7
- 1 John 1:8, 9

Study Questions

- What constitutes betrayal on the part of a Christian?
- Do Christians have a hard time practicing harmony and unity? Why or why not?
- Do you find evidence that God is actively working to redeem and restore humanity? Give examples.
- If animals could talk, what would they say to the church today?

The Manger

"Silence! This meeting will come to order!"

Immediately the large room fell silent. The grand doors opened, and the king entered the Great Hall. A majestic presence, he was tall, imposing, and regal of demeanor. All bowed before him as he passed.

The king sat on the throne and gazed coolly over the assembled crowd that had gathered to attend the General Assembly of Mangers. Here were gathered the most illustrious mangers of all time. What an exciting place to be!

First to present himself was Nabed, a manger from the great city of Babylon.

"I was the favored manger of King Nebuchadnezzar's mighty horses," he proudly announced. As he began to tell of his favored status in the king's stable, an Egyptian manger interrupted him.

"Harrumph! I was the manger for the fabled Arabian chariot horses of the Pharaohs of Egypt," he boasted. Those gathered were awed as they listened to his tales of wonder. They marveled at being in the presence of such historic mangers and delighted at the grand cultural traditions they represented.

But the next manger to announce herself among the resplendent company was even more inspiring. Ooohs and aaahs filled the chamber when the manger from King Solomon's stables stepped forward. Her exotic wood body was overlaid with gold—such extravagance!

"I come from the royal city of Jerusalem," announced the gilded manger. "From me drank only the personal steed of the great and wise King Solomon. And even at that, he was allowed to drink from me only after brushing his teeth."

And so it went. One after the other, mangers from high society and royalty presented themselves to the gathering. Each spoke with pride of their countries, the kings and queens they served, and their favored status as mangers of distinction and privilege. Everyone assembled spoke, except, that is, for a plain and humble-looking manger in a corner of the elegant room. No one had noticed him amid the pomp and circumstance of the occasion. Not until the conclusion of the awards ceremonies did a group of burly mangers take notice of the humble manger.

"Hey, ragtag. Where did *you* come from?" they taunted.

"From Bethlehem, in Judea," replied the manger.

"Har! Did you hear that?" responded one haughty fellow. "But there are no horses in Bethlehem, silly."

At that last comment everyone laughed at the little manger. Even the king was laughing at his expense. And then the most humiliating thing happened. The King ordered that the humble little manger be brought forward so that he, too, could tell his story. This was not because the king was really interested in the unnotable story of an insignificant little manger, but lacking a court jester, he thought it would at least be entertaining.

Trembling, the little manger stepped forward and began to tell his story. He told of his humble beginnings, of being made out of plain and common pinewood. He told of the little backwater town of Bethlehem where he lived. And he described where he lived and served, not in a prince's horse stable, but in a common stable for cattle and sheep. He was, in fact, a common feeding trough for the lowly field animals.

"And this is all your life amounts to?" taunted the king.

"Well, no," replied the humble manger. "The most important thing I've done is to serve as a crib for a baby."

"A baby?" asked the king, puzzled.

"Yes, but this was a special baby—a royal baby," replied the manger in an excited voice.

"Harumph!" responded the king. "If he were a royal baby, he would be laying in a golden crib in a palace. He would not have anything to do with *you*. How dare you tell such a wild story!"

The gathered company of mangers laughed and scorned the humble little manger. Then the king ordered the manger to be put out into the street without finishing his story.

Scripture Study

- Luke 2:7
- Romans 5:8
- 1 Corinthians 1:26-28
- Galatians 2:20

Study Questions

- Is it difficult to recognize greatness in others? Why or why not?
- What are some ways that our culture defines success? What does it mean to have "arrived"?
- If the Christian faith is a counterculture, then what does it mean to be "successful" as a Christian? How do you know you have "arrived" in the Christian life?
- Have you ever thrown out or failed to appreciate something that you later found was of great value? Describe your experience.

The Tree of All Hearts

The night of the big storm was over. By the light of the morning sun Alicia Robin looked all around the courtyard. From her perch on the bench she looked sadly to where the large oak tree that had been her home lay on its side, like a fallen skyscraper. The storm had brought the clouds, cold rain, and terrible lightning that had struck the tree. This had been her parents' home and their parents' home before them. The tree had been home for countless other robins as they returned year after year to build nests and start new families. Now the old oak tree was gone, and so was Alicia's home. She gathered her family together. They all looked so frightened.

"Is our home gone, Mommy?" asked Peter Robin, the youngest.

"Are we homeless?" asked Sarah Robin.

"We don't have a place to live now, Mother!" cried Albert Robin, the oldest.

Alicia tried to look brave, though she felt a little scared, too. "We'll be alright, children. We'll find a new home to live in. It will be a home of our very own."

And so the Robin family started their search for a new home, a place of their own and a place where they belonged.

They did not go far before they came across a poplar tree. "This looks like a nice place," said Sarah. "Let's live here."

But then a puffy gray squirrel peeked out of a hole and said, "You can't live here, this tree is just for squirrels. You don't belong here. Please go away."

Feeling sad, the Robin family kept looking. Soon they came across a maple tree. "This will make a nice house," said Peter. "Let's live here."

Just then a serious-looking owl flew down and said, "No, you can't live here. This maple tree is for owls only. You don't belong here. Please go away."

The Robin family felt hurt. "It feels sad not having a place where we belong," said Sarah.

"Yes, it is sad," said Alicia Robin, "but we must keep looking. We will find a place where we belong."

And so they continued to look. Soon they came across a beautiful pear tree, with lots of branches and beautiful leaves. "This is it! I know it," cried Albert, "This is our new home!"

But just then a small flock of sparrows fluttered around them, yelling, "No, no! This is the sparrow tree. You cannot move here. You do not belong. Please go away."

Alicia Robin felt so sad upon hearing this that she did not know what to do. She was worried about her family and was afraid that she would never find a home for them. She tried to be brave in front of her children, but soon she began to cry.

"Why are you crying?" said a voice. Alicia, Albert, Sarah, and Peter looked. There was a friendly raven, beautiful and black as night.

"We have lost our home," replied Alicia.

"And we don't seem to belong anywhere," said Albert.

"Nobody wants us," said Sarah.

"I know a place where you belong," said the raven, "Come to the Tree of All Hearts. Everyone is welcomed there, and you can have a home among all of God's creatures."

The raven led Alicia and her family across the forest to a beautiful meadow. At its center was the most beautiful tree they had ever seen. It was the Tree of All Hearts. They saw other robins there, along with owls and squirrels and sparrows and all kinds of creatures. They were amazed that they seemed to live happily together, working and playing and worshiping together.

"What is this place?" asked Alicia in wonder.

"This is the Tree of All Hearts," said the raven. "This is the Creator's special tree, where all of God's creatures are welcomed to live and work and worship together under God's rule of peace and love."

"Can we live here?" asked Albert.

"Yes, you can live here," said the raven. "You belong here if you are God's creature. All who love God are welcome here. Welcome to your new home!"

And so Alicia Robin and her family found their new home in the Tree of All Hearts.

Scripture Study

- Acts 9:26-28
- Ephesians 2:11-19
- Acts 15:7-9
- 1 Corinthians 12:12, 13

Study Questions

- Have you ever had to find a new home and a new community? What was the most difficult part of becoming part of a new community?
- Does your church do a good job of welcoming new people into the community? How?
- Have you ever visited a place for the first time that felt like home? Describe it.
- To what extent does God welcome all people home? Are there limitations or exceptions to God's welcoming posture? Why or why not?

The Rock of Ages

"... 7 ... 8 ... 9 ... 10 ... You're out!"

"And the winner by a knockout, in the red corner, the defending Heavyweight Champion of the World, 'The Destroyer!' "

And so went the fight, with the victory going once again to the dreaded reigning champion, "The Destroyer." For eons now he had kept the title, and some sportscasters joked that the title should be renamed for him as "the Invincible Heavyweight Champion of the World." He seemed unbeatable. Indeed, his strength and stamina were known throughout the world. The power of his punches filled even his most powerful opponents with fear.

But the key to The Destroyer's success was not only his strength, but also his cunning. He had more ways of delivering a punch than could be counted. In fact, he seemed to adjust his fight strategy for each opponent, "personalizing" his punches to exploit his opponents' weaknesses. His opponents were left completely destroyed, defeated, and humiliated, with their best defenses totally useless against an enemy who seemed able to read the slightest weakness and ruthlessly exploit it to his advantage.

For example, Adam, David, Solomon, Samson, and many other great men lost their titles to The Destroyer. He used a left hook called "Lust" to defeat them. On Joseph he also used a right cross called "Envy," which almost destroyed the young man. For Eve, Jacob, and the tag team of Ananias and Sapphira he delivered a knockout with his uppercut called "Lie." Balaam and Judas Iscariot lost their fight against The Destroyer when they ran into his devastating right hook called "Love of Money."

But perhaps the greatest fight for The Destroyer, the one that he does not talk about and at times seems strangely forgotten, is his bout with the one known as "The Rock." It was a cosmic fight set in three rounds, witnessed only by celestial spectators.

Round 1: Set in Bethlehem, "The Destroyer" uses the madness of "Political Power," but Jesus, "The Rock" escapes to Egypt.

Round 2: Set in Jerusalem, "The Rock," weakened through fasting and prayer, stands firm against "The Destroyer's" triple threat of "Power," "Doubt," and "Temptation."

Round 3: Set on a hill of death, "The Destroyer" moves in for the kill. "The Rock" is beaten, bloodied, and humiliated; defeat seems certain. "Death" referees the bout and counts to 3 before "The Rock" rises from an apparent knockout and seeming certain defeat.

And now there is one round left for the terrified "Destroyer," who has run out of tricks and moves against the one who stands before him certain of his triumph. Resting between rounds, waiting for the bell that will signal the beginning of his final bout, "The Destroyer" clutches the ropes trembling with fear, white as a sheet. Nothing will deny "The Rock" the final victory. All that remains is to fight the final round and to see it to its predetermined end.

Scripture Study

- Genesis 3:4, 6; 37:4
- 1 Kings 11:1-9
- Judges 16:4-22
- Acts 5:1-11
- Matthew 2:13-18; 4:3-10; 7:24, 25
- Revelation 19:21

Study Questions

- How much of the Christian life is a contest between good and evil?
- Is the outcome of "the fight" in the contest between good and evil assured? Why or why not?
- If God is all-powerful and omniscient, and if the ultimate triumph belongs to God, why is evil such a powerful enemy in our world?
- To what extent do Christians participate in the cosmic contest between good and evil?

A Bug's Light

Once upon a time there was a sad (and sad-looking) little insect who was rejected by all the other bugs. He was not a particularly pretty bug, even by a bug's standards. To be honest, he was a rather ugly little bug. His life was a picture of depression and misery, and he endured his pain alone in the world.

But not everyone "bugged" him, for he did have one friend. One day, when this little bug was feeling particularly low, his friend came and tried to convince him that he was not useless or worthless.

"The problem," he said, "is that you do not know how especially talented you are."

After hearing this, the little bug wanted to cry because he thought his friend was making fun of him. But that was not the case, of course. His friend was sincerely trying to help him, but the more he tried, the more resistance he met from the forlorn bug. It had not been easy to convince Moses that he was the deliverer of God's people, and it was not easy to convince a depressed insect that he was special.

Finally, the faithful friend said, "Tonight, when the night is its darkest, I will return and prove once and for all that you have no reason to be sad."

Night came and, with it, more sadness for the little ugly bug. There was no sign of his friend. He felt lonely, and his thoughts became as dark as the enfolding night. Suddenly, he heard a buzz behind him.

"I thought you weren't coming!" he exclaimed when he saw his friend.

"Oh, yes! I wouldn't miss it for the world," replied his friend. "Watch this!" he cried, and his wings buzzed faster and furiously.

At that moment, and without warning, the friend became pure light. The bug was astounded at what he was seeing.

"Now you do the same!" ordered his friend.

"I can't," replied the astonished bug.

"Yes, you can; you are a firefly."

"But I don't know how," cried the much confused bug.

The patient friend looked at the miserable bug and showed him how it was done. Then he yelled, "Just do it!"

Startled, the little bug followed his friend's instructions. Suddenly, he also became a living, flying light. Who would have thought that this little ugly and seemingly insignificant bug could become a beautiful, shining firefly?

Scripture Study

- Job 25:6
- Psalm 8:4, 5
- Matthew 5:14-16
- Ephesians 5:3

Study Questions

- Do most people have an accurate sense of their personal worth as individuals?
- Is the lack of self-esteem a major problem for Christians? Why or why not?
- Is it true that most Christians do not appreciate their true nature? Explain.
- Have there been moments of "self-discovery" in your life? Share what that was like for you.

Balaam's Mask Store

"Today we have partly cloudy skies, with a 30 percent chance of rain. Our high temperatures will be between 70 and 80 degrees, and the lows in the evening hours will be about 50 degrees. And that's the Channel 6 weather report. Sheila, back to you. . . ."

"Thank you, Ralph. And now let's go to our man on the street, reporter Fred Rumor. Fred is standing by live from Babylon as we continue our series on 'Strange Cities, Strange Places.' Fred . . ."

"Thank you, Sheila. We are in the fabled city of Babylon, standing outside of this unusual mask store called 'Illusions.' Let's go inside and meet the owner."

"And here he is, the owner of Illusions. Hello, sir, I'm Fred Rumor from Channel 6 News, and can you tell us your name?"

"Hello, my name is Balaam, but everyone calls me Beast. Good to meet you. Are we on TV?"

"Yes, we're on TV. That's a camera, and this is a microphone. Tell, me Mr. Balaam, when . . . ."

"Beast. Call me Beast."

"Okay, then, Beast. Could you tell us how long you've been in business at this mask store?"

"Well, Fred, the exact date is hard to pinpoint, but I can tell you that when Abraham the patriarch came through here, the store was already established."

"You knew Abraham personally?"

"Sure! But I never really liked the fellow. He wasn't a regular customer. Only came into the store a couple of times. And when he did, it was only to rent a mask—never to buy."

"How interesting! So tell me, Mr. Balaam, this store rents *and* sells masks?"

"Beast, call me Beast. Yeah, we rent and sell. We even have a lay-away plan."

"I see that in addition to masks you have costumes. These are great for Halloween."

"Well, yes, but we're not a seasonal business, you know. These masks aren't just for Halloween. These are sophisticated and superior masks."

"Oh? What kind of masks do you sell then?"

"Well, we have many categories of masks in our inventory. See here? We have hypocrite masks, super-Christian costumes, sanctimonious saint masks, superspiritual masks, faux Christian masks, and the Judas false-image mask."

"Hmmm. And who are your most common clients?"

"Well, Fred, in general I can say that we have two kinds: false Christians and true Christians who don't want to appear too 'religious'—if you know what I mean."

"And tell me, Mr. Bal . . . er, Beast, how much are these masks?"

"Well, in terms of money, nothing. But there is a price to pay for using these masks. We get great satisfaction at seeing churches in turmoil because of the divisions, hypocrisy, deception, dishonesty, and loss of faith caused by wearing our masks."

"Hmmm. Yes. Well what are your operating hours?"

"We're open 7 days a week, 24 hours a day. People use our masks all the time."

"And what day of the week is your busiest?"

"Saturday nights and Sunday mornings when people are getting ready for church are our busiest times. Sometimes we can hardly keep up with customers then!"

"Well, we've got just a couple of minutes. Any final words for our audience at home?"

"Sure, I'd like to thank all our faithful clients in all the churches out there who've made our business a success. And for you few sincere Christians who've not yet visited our store, come on down!"

"Any plans for the future of Illusions?"

"Yes, as a matter of fact. Because of our success, we plan to expand and franchise our store. Our goal is to have an Illusions mask store next to every local church. That way we can serve our customers better."

"Well, thank you Mr. Bal. . . . er, Beast. You heard it, folks. Watch for the opening of an Illusions mask store near your church soon. Reporting live from Babylon for our series, 'Strange Cities, Strange Places,' this is Fred Rumor for Channel 6 news."

Scripture Study

- Psalm 26:1-4
- Matthew 6:5, 16
- Hebrews 10:22
- 2 Corinthians 11:3-4

Study Questions

- Do most people wear "masks"? Why or why not?
- Is it always wrong to "wear a mask" as described in the story, or is it appropriate at times to "put on a good face"?
- What are some masks you wear? Are there some you wish you did not wear?
- Which of the following is the goal for the Christian life: to wear no masks, to wear fewer masks, or to wear only certain masks?

The Farmer's Dilemma

One day a terrible fire destroyed a farmer's stable, killing many of his animals. The next day torrential rains flooded his farm. After such disastrous misfortunes, he had no choice but to evacuate his beloved farm. Adding to his heartache was the fact that he had room in his trucks for only ten animals—and eleven had survived the ordeal of the past two days that had destroyed their home. Which animals should he choose?

First, the farmer chose his sheep because she was humble, obedient, and provided warmth in the cold nights by providing wool for clothing. Next, the farmer led his donkey into the truck; it was a faithful servant and hard worker. He would depend on the donkey when he started over on his new farm.

Next, he loaded the rooster. The farmer chose him because the rooster had been his "alarm clock" for the past ten years. Every morning without fail the rooster had announced the start of a new day. The farmer could not imagine starting a day in a strange place without the rooster's familiar and hopeful cry.

The farmer kept packing the truck with his precious animals. He chose his faithful dog—a companion and friend—his dependable horse, his milking cow, and his favorite Siamese cat—not a farm animal by any means, but the only luxury he had ever allowed himself to enjoy in his hard life.

He counted seven animals on board. The floodwaters continued to rise, and time was running out. He would have to leave soon to escape being stranded. The next animal he chose was his prized egg-laying hen, and immediately after he picked the goose that would provide the soft warm feathers for his new bed and pillow.

Suddenly, he realized that he had space for only one more animal. It was time to decide who would go and who would be left. The two candidates were a smelly pig and a cute, fuzzy, cuddly rabbit. The farmer did not take long to decide.

"Let's go, pig. You are going with me," he cried.

The surprised and indignant rabbit could not believe his long fluffy ears. He was so much cuter that the pig. He was cleaner and more economical to have around since he certainly didn't eat like a … well, like a pig. Surely the farmer had made a mistake in the midst of his anxiety and of having to leave quickly.

The farmer looked at the rabbit and knew what he was thinking. Sadly, he said, "I really wish I could take you with me, rabbit, but as you can see, I have no more room. You are not obedient like my sheep. Neither are you strong like my donkey. You are so quiet that you can't wake me up in the morning. You are too small to carry me like my horse can, and you don't watch my property like my faithful dog.

"I can't have you sit on my lap because, as you can see, that's the cat's place, and he is very jealous. Furthermore, you can't lay eggs to provide me with breakfast, and your short fur cannot be used to make a downy pillow."

"Very well," said the rabbit. "But what about the pig? Am I not better than him?"

"Listen, rabbit," replied the farmer, "I cannot take you because I have no room for a useless animal. The pig may be ugly and smelly, but he will provide many meals for my family. No, rabbit, I have no use for animals like you that are always hopping from one place to another. All my other animals come when I call, but not you. You jump around in all directions, and I can never get a hold of you. You do not trust me, and I don't need you."

And with that, the farmer drove away with his animals, leaving the rabbit behind.

Scripture Study

- Hebrews 10:2-25
- Luke 17:7-10
- John 15:1-8
- 1 Corinthians 9:24-27

Study Questions

- Have you ever experienced the dilemma of having to choose one valued thing over another? Share that story.
- This story seems to suggest that the farmer made his choices based on his animal's utilitarian purposes. Should this be a guiding value in all decisions? Why or why not?
- Is the worth of persons based on their ability to contribute to society? Why or why not?
- In what ways does God relate to us like the farmer did to his animals? In what ways does God relate differently to people?

Lessons Learned on a Walk

One Saturday evening an aged grandfather and his very young grandchild were ending their day of gentle adventures by walking through their favorite park. Sometimes the young, curious child would talk as they strolled across grass and concrete, and the old man would lean down and respond patiently and with obvious pleasure. At other times neither talked as they walked along, closing the distance between home and the close of the day. Neither was in a hurry to realize the meeting of those two points that would bring an end to their day together.

Suddenly, the young child paused and, pointing to the distance, asked the old man, "Granddad, what do you call those strange looking trees along the road?"

The grandfather looked up and smiled. Amused, he replied, "Those aren't trees, little one; they're posts—posts for power lines."

"Posts? What are they for?" asked the curious youngster.

A former teacher, the grandfather knew the value of seizing teachable moments. He thought for a second before answering. "Those posts hold up power lines, and they are very strong," he began. "It's true that most of them are very old and not too pretty to look at, but looks aren't always important, you know. They may look old and ugly, but those posts are very important."

"Why are they important?" asked the boy as they walked toward a nearby row of power line posts.

"Because they help carry electricity from place to place. Without them, we wouldn't have lights in our house."

"How do they get electricity to our house, Grandpa?" asked the boy.

The old man, falling naturally into the familiar role of teacher, pointed above and said, "See those wires that go from one pole to the other?"

Young eyes followed the gentle bend of the wires stretched between the posts. "Yes," he said, "I see them."

"Good," said the old man, nodding. "Those wires carry the electricity from pole to pole. They go all through the country, the city, the town, and then to our house bringing the electricity with them."

Watching the small boy, the old man thought he could hear his small mind working, trying to grasp the concept. Finally, the child asked, "Grandpa, what would happen if the pole fell down?"

"Well," responded the old man, taken slightly by surprise, "then the electricity would stop, and we wouldn't have lights in the house. But don't worry, those poles are very strong and are planted firmly in the ground. They're like powerful soldiers all lined up that cannot be knocked over."

The young boy persisted, "But what would happen if the wire broke? What then?"

"The same thing would happen," said the old man, convinced that his grandson was the smartest five-year-old on the planet. "We wouldn't have any lights because the electricity couldn't get through. But someone would come to fix the wires right away." He added the last thought quickly lest the boy become frightened; he knew that the youngster sometimes was still afraid of the dark.

They started to amble toward home again, but the young mind was racing. "And where does the electricity come from, Granddad?"

The old man took the young child's hand, as much for comfort as for steadying his gait. It had been a long day, and he was beginning to feel tired. He replied, "The electricity comes from far away, from the power plant. The posts don't make electricity; they just hold up the wires that carry it from one place to another."

"Granddad?" persisted the young boy.

"What?" asked the old man, wondering where this conversation would end.

"Do the wires go all over the whole world?"

"No," replied the grandfather, wondering at the curious question. "No, there are some places in the world where the wires don't reach."

"What happens to the people in those places, Granddad?"

"Well, I suppose the people in those places don't have light. They won't have light until there are enough posts to carry the wires that will bring the electricity."

Staring at his walking feet, the young boy commented, "Then I guess the children there are in the dark, aren't they?"

"I guess so," replied the old man.

A moment of silence passed between them before the youngster said, "You know what, Granddad?"

"What, son?"

"Tonight I'm going to pray that there will be posts all over the world so that everyone can have light."

Scripture Study

- Matthew 5:13, 14; 7:24, 25; 16:18
- 1 Corinthians 12:13-27
- John 1:9; 8:12
- 1 Peter 2:9

Study Questions

- Did you learn any spiritual lessons from a grandparent? What were they?
- This story contains some allegorical elements. What are they?
- In your experience, how insightful are children to the truths of the spiritual life? Explain.
- Who are some people you would consider "strong post" Christians? What makes them this way?

The Empty Crib

There once was a baby crib that was the most beautiful and happy of all cribs anywhere. It was white, clean, and inviting. A tastefully gilded edge gave it an understated, elegant look. But the particular glow that made this the most beautiful crib came not from its gilded frame, but from the joy it radiated from within.

The source of that joy was the sweet tiny baby who slept within. She was the most beautiful baby that had been born that year, and she loved her new crib. It kept her safe and dry and cuddled her to sleep when she was tired. They were both very happy.

But one day sadness cast a shadow over the nursery in which the crib was kept, and over its household. One day I passed by the door of the nursery and heard a sobbing from within. I peeked inside to find that the once elegant crib's luster had faded. It looked miserable and was weeping. I was astounded to see a crib crying and asked, "Why are you crying?"

"Because my little girl, my precious little girl died yesterday," sobbed the crib.

Bravely she told me the tragic story of her sweet girl, whom she once held and protected. She told me of the countless tears and prayers the parents cried on behalf of their precious child. And she told me of the embrace of peaceful eternal sleep that in the end enfolded the baby more completely than human arms or a devoted crib could give.

When she was done telling her tale of sadness and loss, I too was weeping. I cried as I remembered the sweet child, and I wept for the hollow emptiness left for the once happy crib.

Scripture Study

- 2 Samuel 12:18-23
- Hebrews 8:6; 11:40
- 2 Peter 1:4
- Ephesians 5:12
- 1 Thessalonians 4:13

Study Questions

- The death of a child seems to be the most tragic of deaths. Why?
- This story seems to offer no comfort regarding the death of the child. Is this disturbing for you?
- Christians often argue about the "age of accountability" for a child. Is this is a legitimate concern? Why or why not?
- What do we think about prayer in circumstances such as the death of a child? Does it take on a different meaning or function? Does it lose its power?

The Cross-Eyed Brother

Once upon a time there lived a Christian man who had a big problem. Though he was very devoted to God and to ministry, his fellow church members called him the "cross-eyed brother" because of his problem. This was due to the fact that every time a pretty woman would pass nearby, his neck and eyes would snap around to look at her. And if there were two attractive women in the room, his eyes would actually cross as he tried to look at both of them at the same time!

Every day he would ask forgiveness for his wandering eyes and for victory over his fault. But because his heart was not right and his resolve to change was weak, he found no relief in prayer. At times he prayed without faith, and at times he prayed not wanting to believe he could be changed. Truth be told, he was honest enough to admit to himself that he enjoyed his delight in looking at women.

Eventually, however, his frustration at his moral weakness became such that he resolved in a desperate moment that if his prayers for a moral victory were not answered, he would pluck out his eyes!

Sure enough, in a fit of madness born of despair, one dark and desperate evening he went from being cross-eyed to sightless. How he did it no one knows, or cares to imagine. What spiritual pain could cause a person to perform such a bloody and savage act on oneself is best not dwelt upon.

Alas, did his plight improve? Did the desperate act of shutting out light and denying the delight of his eyes cure the lust of the flesh? On the contrary. It is true that he could no longer see the objects of his desires, yet his mind remained fixated on them. In his interior darkness all manner of images crept into his thoughts without the benefit of other distractions—he could no longer shut his eyes or avert his head to escape them.

Scripture Study

- Matthew 5:23, 31
- Proverbs 6:25
- 1 John 2:16
- Hebrews 12:2

Study Questions

- Is there is a real difference between sins committed "in the heart," or "in the mind," and those acted out? Why or why not?
- Does the struggle with temptation and addiction require drastic measures for some people? Explain.
- What is the relation between forgiveness and guilt in this story? Did these forces affect the cross-eyed brother?
- Why do Christians continue to struggle with temptations of the flesh and of addiction?

The Exterminator

"Hello, my name is Pancho Hammer. But around my church and neighborhood they call me 'The Exterminator.'

"No, I'm not a bug fumigator, although I do hate those icky things. And they don't call me 'The Exterminator' because I 'rub out' people, either. What I do is this: I destroy idols of all types, stripes, and sizes.

"You can't imagine what a thrill it is for me to smash and pulverize idols—anything that would take the central place that God alone deserves in people's lives. I've smashed just about anything you can imagine, from religious relics to cars, boats, homes, careers, and unhealthy relationships.

"It all began that day when I first heard about Jesus Christ and his claim to particularity, that as the Son of God only he is worthy of worship and devotion. Overtaken by zeal like the young King Josiah, I went around smashing "idols" everywhere. As you can imagine, this did not go over well with homeowners and the authorities. King Josiah had political connections I did not, and I was soon arrested for vandalism and destruction of private and public property.

"During my time in prison my convictions held firm, but my zeal moderated as I contemplated my past behavior. I learned that violence is not the answer and that you cannot force people to believe differently. This was confirmed when I was released from prison; I saw that all the idols I had so enthusiastically destroyed were merely replaced by others. It was then that I determined to find a way to share the love of Jesus Christ in a more productive and inviting way.

"I found a good church whose members were spiritually mature, patient, and gracious. They taught me how to share the love of Christ in redemptive ways with unbelievers and the idolatrous. I discovered new ways to share my faith, ways more patient and less destructive than I had previously practiced.

"My passion is the same, but my tactics are different. When I meet new believers in Christ, I give them my business card, which reads, 'The Exterminator: Idols Professionally Removed.' If those new Christians desire to remove idols from their lives, then all they have to do is call me. For a reasonable price I provide next-day service, and happily and efficiently remove and destroy all idols and unworthy objects of devotion.

"Now, you would think that I would have a thriving business among the churches. But, sad to say, that's just not so. The idol-removing business is slow work. And it seems to be getting slower every year. Calls come farther apart, and new believers seem to hold on to my business card for a long time before making their first call for extermination.

"Furthermore, I've discovered that my idol extermination business is limited. I can remove idols of stone, gold, metal, wood, copper, silver, and plaster easily. But some idols are beyond my reach. Those are idols of the heart, which can be reached only by prayer, repentance, and the Spirit of God.

"Got any idols you want removed? Give me a call. No job is too small; no task is too large. Satisfaction is guaranteed. And remember, they call me The Exterminator!"

Scripture Study

- Ephesians 5:18
- 2 Kings 23:1-20
- Psalm 96:5
- Isaiah 44:9
- 1 John 5:21

Study Questions

- What is an idol?
- What idols are most prevalent in today's society?
- The Exterminator mentioned that there are "idols of the heart." What might these be?
- If you were to use the services of The Exterminator, what idols would you want him to remove from your life?

No Substitute

On a muggy evening in Chicago the crowds lined up outside the stadium in eager anticipation of being part of history in the making. On that night the final game of one of the most exciting basketball tournaments in memory would decide the team worthy of earning the title "World Champion." Expectations (and wagers) ran high for the game the sportscasters were calling "The Battle of the Titans."

In the home team's locker room, coaches and managers fidgeted and paced nervously, constantly glancing at the clock as the minutes ticked down to the start of the game each of them would remember as the most important of their careers. The head coach gathered his staff for a final briefing. In his heart he knew this action was more to help diffuse some of the jitters they all felt than an actual strategic necessity.

The team physician reported that the team was fit. The players had no injuries to worry about. The assistant coach confidently reported that the morning's practices had gone well.

"The team's ready, Coach!" he cried.

Then the coach turned to the team manager. "How are we on substitutes?" he asked. "Do we have enough?"

"Yes, this year we have enough subs for each position," he responded confidently. But then hesitantly he said, "Except . . ."

"Except for what?!" snapped the head coach.

"Except, we don't have a substitute for Michael," he said wryly. "But then, you know there is no substitute for him!"

The head coach just stared at his manager, not sure whether to chuckle or worry. It was true. How could you substitute for the greatest player the game has ever seen? If any other player were to be injured, he could be replaced. But there was no substitute for Michael, on whom the outcome of that night's game—and the team's hope for victory—weighed heavily.

As this tense scene was unfolding in the locker room, in another place—a site more infernal and deep below the deepest caverns of the earth—another meeting was taking place. This one, however, had a post-game feel to it.

"We've won! We've won!" cried the group of demonic imps who romped around the room. The yells, yips, barks, and grunts—sounds of a warped revelry echoed throughout chambers acrid with the smell of sulfur, decay, and evil.

Suddenly, the din died down as the demon head coach entered the chamber. He was large, tough, mean, and ugly—feared by his otherworldly players and staff as no human coach ever was.

"That's right, you slime," he growled. "We've won! We have completely supplanted the impact of the Enemy's presence in the United States."

The announcement was met with more obscene cheers and vulgar self-congratulatory conflagrations.

The demonic head coach continued with his report. "We have completely substituted Jesus' resurrection with the Easter bunny and colored eggs."

The revelers responded with a hearty "Hooray!"

"We have substituted the spirit of gratitude on Thanksgiving with Turkey Day!"

A louder cheer from the mob shook the rafters.

"And best of all, you worthless lot," bellowed the coach, "we've substituted the celebration of our greatest failure, the Incarnation, with Santa Claus and materialism. Good work all of you!"

And with that last announcement, the damned souls broke out in frenzied celebration of their victory—and why not? They had managed to convince the world that there is a substitute for Christ.

Scripture Study

- 2 Corinthians 3:14
- James 4:12
- 1 John 4:9
- Jude 1:4, 24-25

Study Questions

- Is what Christ provides for people unique, or can there be substitutes for it?
- Have you ever tried to find a substitute for God? Explain.
- Does society at large try to provide substitutes for some of the things God offers? Give examples.
- What are the consequences for those who try to substitute for what God offers?

Gloria and Peace

Once upon a time there were two sisters, one named Gloria and the other Peace. Each was as beautiful as the other. Gloria was the older of the two, a sweet and decent girl who was devout and very dedicated to her faith in God. As often happens in our imperfect world, however, her piety and zeal often brought conflict in her life, for those who would seek the higher and nobler things in life are not spared trouble or pain. And even though Gloria was stunning in appearance, people in general, and men in particular, seemed not to be attracted to her. Behind her back people often commented that they found her demanding, a perfectionist, and even a little fanatical.

On the other hand, everyone loved Gloria's golden-haired sister Peace. She was both admired and desired. She was coquettish and outgoing, but had an ability to put people around her at ease. One look from her, with her deep blue eyes and inviting sunny smile, would make the most anxious person in the room feel tense muscles relax like a gelatin dessert in a warm room.

The problem was that Peace was never at home. Friends, admirers, and suitors came to visit often only to find that she was out somewhere. Gloria, who was always at home, would answer the door to greet the visitors. But none of them stayed long after learning that Peace wasn't at home. After some brief chitchat most would make some excuse to hurry off. Some wouldn't even bother to feign interest or attempt a polite parting; they would simply turn and leave once they learned that Peace was not home. Without so much as a "goodbye," "good day," or a "thank you," they would leave Gloria standing at the door watching their hurried retreat.

Now you would think that Gloria would get her feelings hurt when this happened. But the truth is that this had been going on for so long, she was used to it. Sadly, she had come to expect that no one would ever come to visit her. She was resigned to the fact that she just was not as popular as her little sister—and probably never would be.

One day a young man came to the door looking for Peace (of course). Being the only one at home at the time, Gloria answered the door (naturally).

"Good morning," said the young man. "My name is John Lost. I'd like to see Peace. Is she here?"

As usual, Gloria was kind and hospitable. So, as was her habit, she responded, "Peace is not at home right now, but you're welcome to come in and wait for her." Of course, she never really expected anyone to actually enter the house if Peace weren't there.

But much to her surprise, the young man replied, "Thank you," and actually went in and sat down.

It took a moment for Gloria to compose herself, but soon she had brought out some tea and cookies for the guest and found herself seated across from the young man, Mr. Lost. Feeling awkward at first, they both sipped their tea and nibbled on the cookies. But before long they found themselves engaged in an enjoyable and meaningful conversation. They talked about religion and politics, their likes and dislikes, their families and favorite books, their hopes and aspirations. He shared about his sad past, and she shared about her hopeful future.

During a pause in their conversation Gloria noticed that John Lost was looking at her in a way to which she was not accustomed. Despite her beauty, she was not used to being noticed—especially when her sister was around. Her heart skipped a beat as she almost dared to think that the gleam in John's eyes was . . . love!

And then, incredibly, she heard him say, "You are so beautiful. How is it that no one has fallen in love with you? I can't believe you are here with me. I think I lo . . . ."

He was interrupted in mid-word by a pounding on the door and the sound of a sweet voice crying, "Gloria! Gloria! Open the door! Let me in, I don't have my keys with me!"

It was Peace knocking on the door. With a bit of reluctance Gloria let her in. And the moment she did, Peace became the center of attention, filling the room with her bubbly enthusiasm. John Lost rose from his seat, seemingly mesmerized. Forgetting Gloria, looking at Peace and taking her hand he exclaimed, "You are the one I've been looking for!" And without a word or a backward glance, he put his arms around Peace and swooped her out the door.

Gloria, left standing alone in the middle of the room, felt the tears of humiliation fall silently from her cheek. Once again, someone was stolen away by her sister Peace.

Scripture Study

- Luke 2:14
- Matthew 6:33
- Psalm 34:14; 85:8, 10
- Romans 12:18

Study Questions

- Given a choice, would most people choose the glory of God or the peace of God? Why?
- Is it harder to strive for glory or for peace? Why?
- What is an appropriate definition of peace in the Christian life?
- Is it appropriate for a Christian to desire and seek glory? Explain.

The Rebellious Pillow

I know a man who likes to sleep, although he's not a lazy person by any means. He is responsible, competent, and productive in his work, but he likes his sleep. In fact, he is the only person I know who actually *enjoys* his sleep! Most of us recognize that we need sleep and so tolerate spending a third of our lives sleeping, but this fellow relishes the experience.

Like an enthusiastic hobbyist, he collects those things associated with his passion. He has a comfortable bed specially chosen to meet his standards. His bedroom is designed for comfort and rest, not recreation—no television, stereo, or books by the nightstand for him. Only his favored bed, soft sheets, warm comforters, an embroidered nightcap for cold nights, and soft lights occupy his bedchamber. Oh, and one more thing . . . his pillow.

Now, please believe me when I say that this man is a decent fellow. He enjoys the benefits of a good education and generally is not of a violent disposition. However, if you ever witnessed his evening ritual before falling asleep, you would think him an angry, violent person, perhaps even a little disturbed. You see, every night before falling asleep it's the same thing: after putting on his pajamas and getting under the sheets he tears into his pillow with a fury that would alarm Attila the Hun. He grabs the pillow in his hands, shakes it violently, screams at it, throws it on the bed, thrashes it, punches it, stomps on it, flails at it with his fists, and finally wrestles it to a spot near the headboard where, exhausted, he lays his head on the pummeled pillow and falls into a fitful asleep.

Observing such a strange sight, you would be inclined to think that this man is playing with a few cards short of a full deck. But if you understood the whole story, you'd know that the problem wasn't with the man. The problem was with the pillow!

It all started about six months after he bought the pillow. In the beginning everything was fine. The man had shopped around for just the right pillow. After looking long and hard he found what he thought was the perfect pillow: downy soft on the surface, firm in the middle, luxurious in texture. The pillow was expensive, and he paid more than he should have, but anything was worth a good night's sleep, and this pillow would make for some sweet dreams and a night of blissful slumber. And so it was in those first few months. The man took good care of the pillow, fluffing it every morning without fail, and in return the pillow provided a place of sweet repose for his head.

But the honeymoon lasted only a few months. As the weeks passed, the pillow became rebellious, and that's when the blows started. No matter what position the man placed the pillow, it would move around to a less comfortable spot. The man would fluff it to provide a gentle resting place for his head, but the pillow would create lumps so hard he would wake up in the middle of the night with welts on his face. No matter how hard the man tried, he could not make the pillow conform to his head. In the end the only way either of them got any rest at night was after an exhausting wrestling match. It seems the more the man tries to make the pillow conform, the harder the pillow rebels against him. Theirs is a contrary dance—two souls locked in a battle of wills.

Scripture Study

- 1 Peter 1:7, 13, 19
- 1 Thessalonians 1:9
- 1 Corinthians 6:19, 20
- James 1:2, 3
- Hebrews 12:5-11

Study Questions

- Have you ever been caught up in a battle of wills with someone? Describe the experience.
- To what extent does God try to will us to conform to the desires of God?
- Is it possible to change things by "willing" that they change? Explain.
- In your experience is it a rule that the more you try to exert your will on something or someone to achieve a certain outcome, the opposite seems to happen? Explain.

Edward the Menace

There once was a little boy named Edward. He was a special child, not so much because of any unique gifts or personal characteristics he possessed. No, he was special in the way that all children are special: by virtue of just being a child—a person in the making, holding all the promises of the future and the treasure of things yet to be within the confines of his small self.

His parents, of course, were certain that he was special in other ways. When he was born, they naturally thought he was more beautiful than all the other babies in the nursery. And as he grew, they were convinced that he was more intelligent and talented than his playmates. Being good people, they graciously tolerated the way other young parents gushed over their own children and wondered at how egocentric people can be when it comes to their offspring. They themselves took delight in knowing just how special their child really was, even if no one else seemed able to appreciate it.

In all fairness, it must be said that Edward indeed was a bright child, curious and energetic. In fact, he was *quite* energetic. At first his parents were proud to say that he "went from crawling to running." But soon all that running (and jumping and spinning and trotting and climbing and crawling and hopping and skipping and twirling) got to be troublesome. So full of energy was Edward that his parents were worn out at the end of the day trying to keep up with him.

As he grew bigger and stronger, more and more things around the house were broken or damaged as Edward "got into things." Edward's capricious and energetic ways made for some amusing anecdotes for his parents to tell when in the company of friends and family. There was the time he woke his parents with the explosive staccato sounds of "Foomp! Fooomp! Foomp!" coming from the kitchen. Edward had wanted to make breakfast for his mother and put a dozen eggs in the microwave to make hardboiled eggs (they had scrambled eggs that morning instead). Or the summer he emptied a can of his dad's shaving cream all over the backyard to "make snow." There were peanut butter sandwiches in the VCR, crayons in the blender, pancake syrup in the toaster, the running water hose in the den, the gerbil and the mailman episode (his parents don't talk about that one), the tax returns that were run through the shredder, and other adventures too numerous (or too painful) to recall.

These episodes made for amusing stories, but soon they began to take their toll. It wasn't that Edward was a bad child, just "adventurous and full of life," as his grandparents put it. Edward's constant curiosity and bottomless source of energy became a source of anxiety and frustration for his weary parents. Edward, it turned out, was rather a unique child after all, though in ways his parents had not anticipated.

The biggest frustration Edward's parents faced was that, try as they might to discipline and correct him, Edward didn't seem to be able to learn from it. They got into a pattern: Edward would break something or do something inappropriate, then his parents would correct and discipline him. Edward would respond with a tearful, contrite, and sincere: "I'm sorry. I won't do it again." But his contrition would last all of ten minutes—followed by the next altercation.

"What have you done now, Edward?" his parents would cry.

"Nothing Mom, Dad!" he'd sob. "I'm sorry. I won't do it again!"

Several times during the day the pattern would repeat itself: infraction, discipline, repentance, and the cry of "I won't do it again!" But of course, Edward always did.

Scripture Study

- Exodus 10:17-20
- Deuteronomy 21:18-21
- Proverbs 13:24
- Ephesians 4:12
- Matthew 6:14; 18:21,22

Study Questions

- Why was it so difficult for Edward to keep his promise about changing his behavior?
- Why is it so difficult for Christians to change their poor behavior?
- Which is more effective for helping Christians change their behavior for the better: discipline or patience? Why?
- Have you been successful about making positive changes in your life? How has that come about? What was most helpful to you in making the change?

The Kissing Booth

Excitement gripped the small town just south of Lima, Peru. Rural and isolated, the town of Toratacan was the proverbial "sleepy little town" in the middle of nowhere. Gathering for the daily gossip around the unimpressive but functional fountain in the town plaza was about as much excitement as you could expect. And truth be told, there was not much to gossip about at that. So you can imagine the shockwave of excitement at the big event. The circus was coming to town!

Of course, this was no world-class circus like the Ringling Brothers, but it was pretty decent for its kind—a humble troupe of wandering dreamers, has-beens, perpetually aspiring performers, and lost souls who wandered the backwater towns, bringing to their inhabitants relief from the numbing boredom of small town living. Among its attractions were a large repertoire of "wild" animals (mostly of the domestic kind) that included an aging African elephant; a beautiful Bengal tiger named Zanu; llamas; one very old and tired zebra; and a haphazard collection of dogs, hounds, trained pigs, and performing monkeys.

The stars of this particular company were the once-famous "William the Magnificent" ("El Magnifico"—reportedly once a favorite in the courts of Spain), Edward the sword swallower, and the Amazing Bearded Sandra, who served double duty as the circus strong lady. Sandra had taken over her husband's "strong act" after an unfortunate episode with Evelyn the tattooed lady—but that's another story. The circus also boasted an entertaining company of clowns (who doubled as ticket-takers, carneys, and maintenance personnel).

But by far, the most charming attraction in this traveling circus was the beautiful and sensual Gloria. That was not mere hype; Gloria indeed was one of the most beautiful women ever. In looks she had no equal. When she was in a crowd, heads turned. Young men stammered, and grown men's knees turned to water at the sight of her. Gloria had an easy job in the circus, though it kept her plenty busy. Hers was the most popular attraction in that otherwise inconsequential circus—you could tell by the long snaking line of impatient men leading to her kissing booth!

That's right, for a small fee you could kiss one of the most beautiful women in the world. The price for this privilege wasn't cheap, especially in small towns like Toratacan. But the lines were always long, and no one ever complained. The men of these small towns were known to have spent a week's wages for the mere memory of a kiss from Gloria.

But Gloria was not an easy girl by any means. Paying a steep price for the privilege of kissing her wasn't enough. Gloria insisted on one condition before she allowed any man to kiss her: He needed to have brushed his teeth, but more specifically, he must not have bad breath. Before she allowed a customer to kiss her, she would sniff his breath. If he had not brushed his teeth, and if his breath was not fresh, she would send him away with the admonition: "Brush your teeth and clean your breath!"

On the first day of the circus' visit to Toratacan, who was first in line at the kissing booth but old Boniface, the town's barber. The night before he had emptied his till, dug up from his backyard the old coffee can that contained his "retirement fund," and bought a ticket for the kissing booth. Then early in the morning, before the rooster and the sun made their appearance, he planted himself below the window of the kissing booth in eager anticipation. Can you imagine his dismay, then, when after gazing at the beautiful Gloria with his lips puckered, he heard her say, "Brush your teeth and clean your breath!"

Devastated, but undaunted, Boniface rushed back home and scrubbed his teeth—twice! Then he ran all the way back to the circus grounds and stood at the end of the long line for Gloria's booth. After a two-hour wait he was again in the presence of this woman of his dreams. He plopped down his ticket, closed his eyes, leaned forward, puckered his lips, and heard, "Brush your teeth and clean your breath!" He could hardly believe his ears!

"But I brushed my teeth!" he protested, "Twice!"

Gloria's assistant pulled Boniface out of the line and inspected his teeth. Sure enough, they were pearly white and gleaming, but he still had bad breath.

"Listen, Boniface," the assistant whispered in confidence, "you seem like a nice guy, so let me tell you the secret to having fresh breath. Would you like to know?"

"Yes! Please tell me," pleaded Boniface.

"You see," said the helpful assistant, "it's not enough to just to brush your teeth; you have to brush your tongue, too."

"My tongue?!" puzzled Boniface.

"Yes, whenever you brush your teeth, you must brush your tongue also. It's the only way to get rid of bad breath and have a clean mouth," instructed the assistant. "Now, do you want to get to kiss the beautiful Gloria or not?"

"Yes, I do!" he cried desperately.

"Then go brush your tongue, and afterward come back."

Scripture Study

- James 1:22-25
- James 3:3, 5, 11
- Colossians 3:17; 4:6
- Isaiah 6:1-8

Study Questions

- Why do you think words have such power to hurt and to heal?
- Have you ever been hurt because of something someone said about you? Have you ever been "blessed" by something someone said about or to you? Explain.
- What would be the spiritual equivalent of brushing one's tongue as opposed to merely brushing one's teeth?
- Should a Christian's speech be different than that of non-Christians? How?

A Winning Plan

"A doctor! Help! Someone please call a doctor."

This was the heartbreaking cry of an anguished mother as she leaned over her son Thomas, who was lying injured on the pavement. Another attack from a youth gang left him as yet one more victim of his neighborhood violence.

This was not the first time Thomas had been beaten by local gangs. Thomas was young and brave, and he fought back to defend himself from the bullies, but he was always beaten and humiliated. The problem was that Thomas was thin and weak. His muscles were stringy from lack of exercise, and he suffered from the effects of malnourishment due to a poor diet.

"This can't go on," Thomas said to himself one day. "Things must change! I'm tired of getting beat up."

And so, with newfound determination, Thomas joined a gym as soon as he recovered from his wounds. With the help of his doctor he started a new diet that included balanced nutritional meals and vitamins. His trainer put him on a high protein supplement to build his muscles.

By the end of the year Thomas was a different person. He was taller, bulkier, stronger, and confident. Instead of being a target for the local bullies, he was the terror of the block to anyone who would pick on a weaker person. No one dared take him on! In addition to being physically intimidating, he hung around some of his friends from the gym, who were ready to defend him from any threat from the local gangs.

Naturally, Thomas' newfound strength—both physical and emotional—did not come easy. He sacrificed a lot to get to where he is today. He worked out, no longer sat around watching TV, quit eating sweets and empty calories, and ran twice a day. He stopped going to parties, missed a summer vacation, and gave up any vice or bad habit that detracted from his goal. But in the end all those sacrifices paid off, and having reached his goal, he realized he did not miss any of the things he gave up.

Scripture Study

- Hebrews 12:2
- 1 Peter 5:3
- 1 Corinthians 9:24
- 2 Timothy 2:7

Study Questions

- Are there spiritual exercises a Christian must practice to remain spiritually fit? If so, what are they?
- Is it possible to get spiritually weak from a lack of physical exercise? From a lack of spiritual exercise?
- What sacrifices might a Christian have to make in order to stay spiritually fit?
- If someone asked you to be their spiritual personal trainer, what kind of exercise program would you start them on?

The Skinny Mouse

This is the story of three mice, who just happened to be brothers. They lived a happy existence with their mother mouse and father mouse, who provided for them and taught them well in the ways of mice. They lived in a house perfectly suited for mice; the owners seemed either not to notice their existence or not to care. There was always plenty of food laying around and enough clutter in every room for the mice to move about freely, hiding behind one pile or another of stuff as they made their way throughout the house in search of left-overs and crumbs.

One tragic day the parents of the three young mice ventured out-side the house only to encounter a stray cat. Being plump and well-fed mice, they had no hope of outrunning the cat. They were eaten lick-ity-split, never to be seen again.

The three mice brothers were sad about their loss, of course. But they were well into their adolescence, and so determined that it was just as well to move on with their lives. Cheering each other on, they decided they would go out to make their fame and fortune in the world. Furthermore, they made a pact that one-year hence, they would meet again in the old cluttered house that had been their home all those happy years. At that time they would share their fortunes and tell of the great adventures they had on the way to glory and fame. With that solemn promise, they embraced each other and went their separate ways.

One year passed, and true to their promise, the three brother mice gathered in their old home for a reunion. They greeted each other with glee, squeaking with joy as only happy mice can. The older brother happily shared news of his year away. He had become a movie star, playing mouse roles in Hollywood movies. He told about the glamorous lifestyle he loved and about all the celebrities he had worked with. Best of all, he got paid in cheese! Living a life of luxury, he had grown plump and fat.

The middle brother shared about his success as a "refuse man-agement engineer." He worked in one of the largest landfills in the world where, as he liked to put it, he sat "on top of the world." With mountains of leftovers, trash, and garbage at his disposal (no pun intended), he too had grown plump and fat.

The two older brothers rejoiced seeing that they each had fulfilled their dream of "making it" in the world. And there is no better sign of that for a mouse than to be plump and fat. And while they were happy for each other, they were surprised and saddened to see that in the course of their year apart, their little brother mouse had become thin, pale, and nervous.

"What happened to you?" they asked eagerly.

The skinny mouse told his sad story. It seems that the day his brothers left the house to find their way in the world, the little mouse looked around him and decided that he could not do better than stay where he was. This was the ideal place to be, he decided. He had plenty of food and a house he liked. He had no need to leave the house he grew up in since he had everything he needed.

For some months life was good. He had run of the house and plenty of food to eat since the owners of the house were very sloppy housekeepers. They left food all over the house and never cleaned up. It was a mouse paradise!

But one day things changed. For some unknown reason the owners of the house started to clean up. They picked up the trash around the house, cleaned the walls, and scrubbed the floors. They no longer left piles of stuff around, so the mouse found that he could not get around as easily as he once had. As the cleaning project continued, there was less and less food to eat. After a few weeks there was not a single crumb left in the now spotless kitchen! Luckily, the mouse had stored some food in his little mouse hole behind the cupboard. He was able to live off of that for a while, but soon that ran out, too. For the first time he began to feel hunger.

To make matters worse, the family continued their newfound passion for cleanliness. Not only did they keep the house clean, but they also brought in a professional pest control company to deal with pests in the house. (Like the skinny mouse, several still hung around, hoping the family would return to their old ways). The exterminator put out traps and poisoned pellets of food, and even fumigated the place.

Being a smart little mouse, the younger brother avoided the traps and did not eat the poisoned food—tempting though it was. But when the fumigation began, he had to run out of his hiding place behind the cupboard to be able to breath. Feeling sick and weak, he wandered out onto the kitchen floor only to encounter an even worse danger: the owners had bought a cat! For a second he was paralyzed with fear, then he ran across the spotless kitchen floor as fast as he could. Despite his weakened condition, he was able to get away from the horrible cat, but not without first being pounced on and batted around at least twenty times.

Now the little skinny mouse stayed in his miserable little hole behind the cupboard all day, hungry, weak, and afraid to venture out. The older brothers stared at the skinny mouse with great pity. Then they looked at each other and back at the little mouse and asked, "But why did you stay?"

Scripture Study

- 2 Peter 2:10-22
- Genesis 19:17, 26
- 1 Kings 19:1-4, 9-12
- 1 Samuel 17:11, 23-27

Study Questions

- Do you remember setting out to "conquer the world" at some stage in your life? Share your experience.
- Do most people choose comfort over adventure; security over risk? Why or why not?
- Why do some people remain in unhappy or undesirable situations?
- What, if anything, would have motivated the skinny mouse to leave his home? Explain.

Philip and the Blackbird

It was a lovely morning, fresh and calm. The sun, just peeking over the horizon, spread its light on the new day, washing both the God- and manmade world with a hue that gave it a subtle harmony. Philip awoke in accord with the spirit of newness in the air. He went through his morning routine—shower and shave, breakfast, Bible reading, sports page—in a peaceful frame of mind.

He shrugged on his backpack and retrieved his bike from the garage. With headphones in place he started his usual twenty-minute ride to work. Riding to the office not only saved him money, which was a primary motivation for this sweaty and sometimes hazardous mode of transportation, but he actually enjoyed the exercise and the quiet morning ride.

He settled into his usual routine, going over his accustomed route through the familiar neighborhood streets, the highway overpass, the access road, then through the park. The only traffic he encountered was on the last five blocks before arriving at the building where he worked. In his mind he was already there, sitting at his desk with his first cup of coffee of the day (at home he always had juice, cereal, and a bagel for breakfast). But today something happened that shattered Philip's comfortable routine forever.

Just after entering the park Philip unconsciously slowed down, as was his habit. There was something about riding through this little oasis in the middle of town that made him want to slow down and enjoy the trees, fountains, and gentle grassy slopes. But just as he circled around a bend near a large ancient oak tree, Philip was startled by a "swoosh!" The violence of the sound and the gust of wind that hit his cheeks were enough to cause him to wobble his front tires, causing his left foot to slip off the pedal. "What could that have been?" he asked himself.

Philip looked behind him in time to see a huge blackbird swooping down on him. Another swoosh left his veins feeling like they were filled with ice water. His chin hit the handlebars as the bird pulled up from a dive-bombing maneuver.

"What's the matter with that crazy bird?" Philip cried, as he ped-dled like mad to escape. His heart was pumping hard, his leisurely routine broken. He would feel stressed all day. The blackbird made two more passes at Philip before letting him go.

This morning encounter repeated itself for several days. Entering the park was no longer something to look forward to; just approach-ing the gates filled Philip with anxiety. His co-workers started to notice that Philip was nervous and jumpy at work, as if he wasn't get-ting enough sleep or was nervous about something.

Finally, out of concern, one of his co-workers asked Philip how he was doing. Relieved to be able to share his anxiety and surprised at his lack of embarrassment, Philip told of his misadventures with the blackbird in the park and about how his cherished morning routine had been shattered.

"You know what I think, Philip?" asked his co-worker. "I think that bird is just hungry."

"You think so?" asked Philip. "You don't think he's got it in for me?"

"No, I don't think it's personal," replied the helpful co-worker, amused. "I'll bet if that bird finds something to eat, it will leave you alone."

Philip thought about what his co-worker suggested. The next day he set out on his bike again, but this time he had a plan. As soon as he entered the park, Philip pulled out a slice of bread from his back-pack. Peddling past the oak tree, he dropped pieces of bread behind him. Expectantly, he watched as the large blackbird that had tor-mented him all week flew off his perch in the tree. Philip watched with alarm as the blackbird flapped violently toward him. Feeling his chest tighten with terror, he tossed aside the rest of the bread and pumped his legs as hard as he could.

Anxiously looking over his shoulder, expecting another close encounter with the dive-bombing bird, Philip was surprised to see that the bird had not pursued him after all. Stopping his bike, he looked back to see the blackbird feeding on the pieces of bread he had dropped behind him. His plan had worked. Feeling both excitement and relief, Philip watched the bird for a few minutes. The once vio-lent blackbird ate away at the bread, ignoring Philip altogether. With a feeling of triumph Philip turned and rode away whistling. This was going to be a good day.

Scripture Study

- Matthew 28:20
- John 6:35-39
- Romans 8:37
- Philippians 4:13

Study Questions

- To what extent is the following phrase true: "The only thing we have to fear is fear itself"?
- What three things do people fear the most? Explain.
- What three things do *you* fear the most? Explain.
- Has fear ever held you back from attempting or accomplishing something? Explain. Did you ever overcome your fear?

The Prideful Cigar

The president of a certain country was a man of unusual political talent. He was energetic, a master communicator, and a charismatic leader. He was acknowledged as a man of wisdom and diplomacy by both admirers and detractors. An efficient administrator, he had realized all of his campaign promises. All these qualities helped to make him one of the most beloved and popular presidents his country had ever known.

Like all mortal men, however, this beloved president carried within him personal faults and flaws. Among them was a particularly unfortunate vice: the president loved to smoke cigars. The overwhelming bitter odor of his favorite imported cigar followed him about as he went from meetings to political events. During staff meetings an oppressive blue cloud hung over the conference table with varied and unfortunate effects on the presidential staff. And no matter what the housekeeping staff tried, they couldn't get the smell of cigar smoke out of the drapes and carpeting of the presidential dwelling. Despite all the inconvenience and embarrassment that the president's bad habit caused, no one dared to broach the subject with him.

One day the president's wife summoned her courage and decided that for his health's sake, and for the sake of his political career, she needed to confront him about his bad habit. With great tact she explained to him her concern of what smoking cigars was doing to his health. She related how his staff patiently suffered through meetings because of the smoke, though privately it would be a topic of complaint to the Chief of Staff. She shared about how such a public vice was affecting his political image and popularity.

Being a wise man and a sensitive husband, the president carefully considered his wife's concerns. Seeing the truth in what she had pointed out, and for the sake of his country, he conceded that he had a problem. With the help of his good wife and a few trusted friends, the president devised a plan to help him overcome his bad habit.

Across town, at the same moment that the president was taking action to change his ways, in a particularly upscale cigar store—

considered by the country's smoking aficionados to be the best cigar store in the country—a curious conversation took place in the few hours before opening time.

"I am the best cigar in the world!" boasted one of the prized cigars in the store. It was thick, aged to perfection, almost a foot long, and prominently displayed with care behind a glass case.

The other cigars tried to dismiss his boasts. They made fun of his ornate gold-leafed band and ostentatious vanity, but secretly, many of them were envious. Despite the fact that the cigar's boasting was unseemly, it indeed was a magnificent piece of work. Even some of the elite cigars in the store were jealous of the pride the storeowner took in displaying his find.

"You'll see," carried on the prideful cigar. "I am destined to be smoked by the rich and famous. Why, even the president would be lucky to have me!"

Later that morning a very distinguished man entered the store. His bearing and demeanor left no doubt that this was a man of status and power. Anyone who doubted this man's importance was soon dissuaded upon seeing the entourage that followed him: a secretary, a couple of minor but recognizable celebrities, a half dozen staffers, and several large and severe-looking men in dark suits with a no-nonsense way of taking over any room they entered.

"Good day, Mr. President!" stammered the shopkeeper, trembling with both surprise and nervousness. The owner of this fine establishment had a standing agreement with the president's office. Every month he would send a box of fine cigars to the president, but this was the first time he had ever laid eyes on the famous and beloved leader of his country. This was something he never dreamed would happen—the president paying a visit to his cigar shop!

"What can we do for you sir?" he managed to ask after a few uncertain seconds.

"I want to purchase one of your fine cigars," replied the president. "In fact, I want to buy the best cigar you have in your fine store."

Without hesitation the storeowner hurried to the case that held the prideful cigar that only a few hours before had made the rash boast that was now coming true. Taking it carefully out of the case, the owner handed the cigar to the president.

"Here it is, Mr. President," said the storeowner with obvious pride. "This is the best cigar in the world."

The prideful cigar turned to his companions and said, "See? Didn't I always say I was the best? Didn't I say I'd be famous some day? I told you so. The president himself came for me."

The next day the president gathered an assembly of his cabinet, the house staff, friends, and media. Hundreds of people were gathered in the great hall to listen to a special announcement the president promised. All present thought that this event must be about something very important, because rarely would such a mixed and large company gather for an official announcement. So you can imagine everyone's surprise when they heard the president's first words.

"My fellow citizens," he began. "Today I want to talk to you about my cigar—the greatest cigar in the world."

The crowd was stunned. Had the president gone insane? Was he ill? Did he really gather this great assembly to talk about a cigar? Did he not realize what a controversial and sensitive issue this was to all gathered?

The president made a big show of rolling the thick cigar between his fingers, holding it up to his ear to listen to the freshness of its crinkle, then holding it under his nose and breathing deep the rich aroma of its selected and well-blended tobacco leaves. Then, with great flourish he lit the cigar, and with obvious pleasure breathed in a lungful of thick aromatic smoke.

What pride the boastful cigar felt at that moment! Oblivious to the tension in the room—since as far as he was concerned the whole occasion centered around him—the cigar billowed a thick flume of smoke that filled the room with a blue (and smelly) mist as it wafted over the heads of the crowd.

The president exhaled, filling the room with more smoke, then held the cigar over his head. The boastful cigar was in seventh heaven. Such acclaim! Such recognition!

Staring at the cigar overhead, the president cried in a loud voice, "From this day on, and forever more, I will never smoke another cigar as long as I live."

With that the president threw the surprised cigar to the marbled floor, stepped on it, and ground it into a pile of ash and ground tobacco leaves. With obvious pleasure he stomped on it twice for added good measure.

A cheer went up in the room. This was indeed good news, worthy of national attention. Amid great applause several of the important guests symbolically stomped on the now stunned and humiliated cigar—including the first lady. Guest after guest, having suffered years of the president's former vice, joined in on the stomping, till at the end of the evening all that was left of the once boastful cigar was a stump. Adding insult to injury, one staff member yelled, "Get that stogie out of here!"

As the guests retreated to a victory reception, a janitor swept up the remains of the cigar that only yesterday was seated in a glass-enclosed velvet container. Walking outside to the rear of the presidential residence, underneath a window from which could be heard the festivities, the lowly janitor sat down on a wooden crate, brushed off what was left of the cigar, and with a common wooden match lit the stump and leaned back for a good smoke.

Scripture Study

- James 4:10
- 2 Chronicles 26:16-21
- Psalm 10:4
- Proverbs 11:2; 16:18

Study Questions

- The proverb says that "pride goeth before the fall." What does that mean? Do you believe it?
- Is pride always a bad thing? Is pride always a sin?
- What is the relationship between pride and positive self-esteem?
- Has anyone ever said to you, "I'm proud of you"? Who? How did you feel?

The Living Tree

"What a beautiful tree! Where did you get it?"

"I got it on one of my travels through the Middle East," responded the proud host, pleased with the reaction of his guest.

The tree in question was no ordinary tree. It indeed was a beautiful fruit tree—lush, bursting with vibrant green leaves with branches full of plump fruit. But the extraordinary thing about this particular tree was that on every branch grew a different kind of fruit. With the forty different kinds of fruit it bore, the tree resembled a Christmas tree with hundreds of large, colorful ornaments.

It was a fantastic tree and gave its owner (a budding horticulturalist) great delight to see the surprised looks on the faces of his guests. Every visitor to his fantastic gardens left amazed at the tree of many fruits. But only for his special guests did the host allow the pleasure of seeing his *most* amazing tree. Yes, as fantastic was the tree with forty fruits at which the guest now gaped, there was one tree even more amazing still.

The host led his guest further into his garden and pointed to a tree similar in kind to the amazing multiple fruit-bearing tree. But the tree he pointed at with obvious pleasure had only one kind of fruit on its branches. Compared to its sister tree, this one looked rather common.

The excited host pushed his guest toward the tree and said, "Taste this fruit. You won't believe how delicious it is."

The curious guest reached into the branches and grabbed a large, ripe-looking fruit. It felt full and plump to the touch, but try as she might, she couldn't pull the tempting fruit off the branch.

"Try another one," said the chuckling host.

Determined, his guest reached for another fruit and gave it a yank. But it, too, stayed on the branch. No matter how hard she pulled, the fruit would not come off the tree.

Before his guest became too frustrated, the host explained that unlike the other tree of many fruits, this tree's fruit never fell. Once a fruit appeared on the branch, it remained connected to the tree forever.

"How is that possible?" cried the guest. "And what good is it? How can someone enjoy the fruit if it doesn't come off the tree?"

The owner of this unusual tree turned to his guest and asked, "Do you want to know the secret for enjoying the fruit of this tree?"

"Yes!" cried the bemused woman. "Please tell me."

"If you want to taste the fruit from this tree, you'll have to eat the fruit directly from the branches without picking the fruit or cutting it down. But be prepared; you have never tasted anything like it."

Skeptical, but overcome with curiosity, the guest approached the tree, stood on her tiptoes, and took a bite from a fruit on a low-hanging branch. The taste was fabulous. It tasked like a peach, but richer and sweeter than any peach she'd ever tasted.

"Have another bite," encouraged the host, with a mischievous gleam in his eye.

The guest did so, and to her amazement the next bite from the same fruit tasted like a succulent apple. Another bite tasted like a pear, and the next tasted like a mango, and the one after that tasted like a melon. Bite after bite tasted like a different fruit altogether: pineapple, strawberry, orange, banana, kiwi, tangerine, apricot . . . . As amazing as that was, the guest almost fainted when, taking a pause between bites, she noticed that the fruit was not being consumed: after each bite it would return to its original shape, looking as if it had never been touched!

"What's going on?" cried the guest. "How can this be?"

"Observe," commanded the host, "and watch carefully."

They moved to the other side of the tree where the excited guest noticed a large root stretching from the trunk of this tree to the other amazing tree in the garden, the tree of many fruits. This thick root connected the two trees in such a way that she intuitively realized that these were not two trees after all—they were the same tree!

"Sit here and keep watching," whispered the host.

They sat on the soft grass and watched. After some time the guest noticed that one of the fruits fell from the tree of many fruits. Instead of landing on the ground with a thud, it flew across the field and attached itself to the branch of a dry barren tree.

"Now look carefully, and you will learn the secret of my wonder-ful groves," cried the host, pointing to the dead tree.

The stunned guest watched and to her amazement saw the old dead tree shimmer with a warm light for a brief moment. It shook and creaked, and then within minutes turned as lush in color and life as the original tree of many fruits. The guest watched as this process repeated itself: a fruit would drop from the branches of the amazing tree, fly and attach itself to a dead tree in the orchard, and then that tree would come to life.

Finally, the guest turned to her host and asked, "What can this mean?"

Scripture Study

- John 15:4-7, 16
- Galatians 5:22, 23
- Psalm 1:2, 3
- Luke 6:44
- Colossians 1:6, 10

Study Questions

- How would you answer the last question the guest asked?
- This story contains allegorical elements. What do the various elements in the story represent?
- Trees are powerful universal symbols in stories. What might a tree represent?
- If you were able to plant a fantastic and magical tree in your garden, what might that tree be? What kind of fruit would it produce?

The Best Dad

On a quiet afternoon, during a lull between their usual games of catch and basketball and bike riding, a group of boys sat around a front yard drinking lemonade. Soon, discussion turned to the topic of who had the best father.

One of them said, "I have the best dad. He works day and night with his hands to buy us everything we need."

Another responded, "No, *my* dad is the best because he helps us with our homework every evening after dinner. And on the weekends he takes us out somewhere to have fun together."

A third countered, "That's cool, but my dad does much more. He hugs us and shows us that he loves us very much. He cares a lot for us and spends a lot of time with us. He even plays video games with us, even though he always loses."

And so the argument about who had the "best father" continued. Each boy mounted argument upon argument as to why his dad was the best. The boys talked of gifts, allowances, time spent with them, participation in sports, important jobs, salaries, trips, and the usual things boys appreciate about dads.

All of a sudden they became aware of how quiet their friend Alex had been during this discussion. Alex was an orphan but, although shy, was often talkative with his group of friends. After his father's death he had become a bit withdrawn, and his circle of friends was small but meaningful. Boys being boys, they decided to make Alex the arbiter of their debate, unaware of how uncomfortable the subject of dads can be to a boy who does not have one.

"So tell us, Alex," one of them prodded, "who do you think has the best dad?"

Alex stared back for a moment, annoyed that his friends could not see or understand the hurt he'd been feeling as he listened to them talk about their dads. He looked at each of them, then said, "Me. I have the best dad."

Some of the boys laughed, and some sneered. "How can you say that? You don't even have a dad," taunted one of them.

Alex just looked at them and said, "I have the best dad in the whole world. He is never too busy for me. He provides everything I ever need or deserve. He watches over me constantly, cares for me, and is always there when I need to talk to him. He disciplines me when I've done wrong, but best of all, he loves me so much that he gave a life for mine. He promises me that I will always be in the embrace of his arms of love. He's the best dad!"

Scripture Study

- Matthew 28:19, 20
- John 15:13
- Romans 5:8; 8:32
- Galatians 2:20
- Ephesians 5:2

Study Questions

- What qualities make for a great dad?
- To what extent can you identify with God as Father? Is this a positive or negative image for you? Why?
- Are humanlike metaphors and expressions of God limiting, or are they the highest understanding of God we can have?
- If you were to write this story from a feminine point of view, with a group of girls sharing about the "best mom," how would the story be different?

The Race to the Finish

In a central European city one of the most challenging and prestigious sporting events in the world was taking place. Thousands of athletes from all over the world gathered in this ancient city to take part in the world-renowned Super Marathon, an event that had such grueling demands on even the fittest of athletes that the winner would be celebrated as the "greatest athlete in the world."

Among those who took the challenge this year were the two most favored to win the race: from Italy, Bruno Campeoni; and from the Ukraine, the popular hero of his small village, Sergei Rapidoski.

After much readiness and anticipation the lineup formed, the starting gun sounded, and the race started. Sergei quickly jostled for a spot among the leaders and maintained his lead over the pack for the first 30 kilometers. Bruno, on the other hand, found his pace, firm but not too aggressive or rushed. As an experienced runner, he knew his body and his limitations. He allowed his practiced body to find its own rhythm, knowing he would need some energy in reserve for the final leg of the race.

At the 35-kilometer mark more than half of the runners had abandoned the race. Some runners had simply quit, some were injured, many had no energy left, and several suffered physical trauma severe enough to warrant medical attention. This was not the most action-packed sporting event of the year, but it was not without its drama. Would a runner fail due to a lack of will or a lack of strength? Would it be a failure of nerve or a failure of physical athletic ability that would determine the fate of a competitor?

The obstacles were many: distance, the press of the crowd, hills and rough terrain, heat, fatigue. In addition, at one point the runners encountered a freak torrential downpour with gusting winds that made every step twice as hard and made breathing almost impossible. The best runners put their chins to their chests and drove on through pain and exhaustion; others succumbed to this unexpected challenge as the final insult to an already nearly impossible goal.

By the time the runners reached the 40-kilometer marker there were only 500 athletes left in the race. But from that point on, the racers accelerated to a frenetic pace. Spectators marveled that anyone could find a source of energy to call forth from the exhausted and battered bodies.

Bruno stepped up his pace and dramatically pushed ahead of the others. The runners were astonished and crushed at the way he slowly pulled away from them. Devastated, most gave up the race—emotionally, if not physically—as soon as he passed them. Soon Bruno could see only Sergei and two other runners ahead of him.

Now the 41-kilometer marker was in sight. Once the runners passed it there would be only 1 1/2 kilometers left to the finish line. Bruno redoubled his effort, and with a burst of speed that left the spectators gasping in amazement he charged toward the finish line. All eyes were fixed on this marvelous athlete. All over Europe a collective cry rose, "Bruno! Bruno! Bruno!"

Victory was imminent for the favored Italian hero. But suddenly, disaster struck. As Bruno sped past the astonished Sergei on his way to the finish line, he tripped! Sandwiched between the other two runners who had paced just behind Sergei, the three exhausted athletes tumbled to the ground in a tumbling heap of arms, legs, groans, and tears.

The world watched in despair as Sergei ran ahead toward the finish. Bruno lay on the ground as runners who had been left behind ran past him. Moments passed, and soon runner after runner crossed the finish line as Bruno lay on the ground where he fell.

"It's over," thought every spectator who watched this tragic episode. All those years of training, the countless hours of sacrifice and pain, and then the marvelous performance that had proven Bruno a world champion—it had been for nothing. He had been so close, victory was within reach, then a misstep, and it was all over.

But true champions never quit. They may fall, but they always rise again and finish the race. And Bruno was a true champion.

With the help of some sympathetic runners who were just getting near enough to the finish line to see their goal, Bruno got to his feet. Injured and in pain he set his face toward the finish line and trotted toward it. There was no grace or speed in his movements. Step by step he plodded toward the finish line—stumbling, shaking, weaving.

Some could not bear to watch this spectacle; many could not decide if it was the act of a true athlete or a fool. One hour after the end of the race, long after the awards ceremony, long after the cameras and the sportswriters had left, Bruno crossed the finish line.

Scripture Study

- Hebrews 12:1
- Galatians 5:7
- 2 Timothy 2:5
- 1 Corinthians 9:24-27

Study Questions

- What is the difference between being nobly persistent (never giving up) and being a fool?
- How is the Christian life like a race?
- Have you ever strived for something and gotten very close to achieving it, but then did not realize your goal? Share your experience.
- How important is it to finish first? Is it just as important simply to finish?

Why Families Fight

"There it is!" cried the team leader of the band of demons and gremlins as it pointed to the quiet little house on a typical suburban street.

The ghastly group climbed out of their ghost truck and surrounded the house. The team leader double-checked the name on the mailbox against the list on his clipboard. "Yep, this is it," he said. "We're early. We'll have to wait a few minutes. Smoke 'em if you got 'em," he barked.

The motley group cursed and groaned. They were eager for some action, and waiting was not a virtue of this crowd. They sat around the outside of the house, slumping on the steps, sitting on top of the rose bush (the roses near the top of the bush quickly withered into a sad, gray-brown, paper-thin mass), leaning against the mailbox on the front lawn. Inside, the unsuspecting family members went about their usual activities that filled the lull before dinnertime.

After a few minutes a car pulled into the driveway, and the team from the Netherworld yipped and howled. The man of the house—husband, father, and breadwinner—was home after a long hard day's work, and the fun was about to start. The team leader grinned mischievously as he waited for the man to get to the front door. Just as the man turned the key to enter his house, the demon leader cried, "Go!" And with that they began the carefully planned assault on the unsuspecting Christian household of the Rogers family: husband, wife, and three children.

He was a deacon in his church and a good husband and father. She taught Sunday School and volunteered in the church pantry, feeding the poor. The kids were wholesome, if unremarkable. They played sports, were interested in music, were obedient and respectful of their parents and other adults. They were the kind of children who could make the children's and youth programs of any church a success by their faithful participation and support.

The first to attack was Apagon, a dark demon who surrounded the environs of the house with an oppressive cloud of spiritual darkness. Normally this cloud could snuff out all passions and leanings toward the spiritual, but in this Christian home all it managed to do was suppress a level of Christian joy usually experienced by the family. No matter, however, for this was merely a preparatory tactic to weaken them for the full assault.

As soon as Apagon finished its work, in rushed Confusion and Griton. These two headed straight for the children. Unseen, they pinched and prodded, nudged and tweaked, and within minutes the children found themselves whining, fighting, and running around the house yelling and screaming.

The anxiety in the house was building as the first assault wave took its toll. But this group of devils wasn't through yet. Next into the fray was the one called Criticon. Its specialty was to get under people's skin and cause tongue wagging.

"What have you done all day?" asked the man with more criticism in his voice than he intended.

The comment found its mark. Hurt and confused, the wife snapped, "Me? Sleeping and watching TV, what do you think?" The sarcasm in her voice surprised her, but at the same time it released some of the growing tension in her throbbing temples (where two little imps where digging their sharp claws).

The attack was in full swing. For fifteen minutes the demons and imps kept up their strategy of prodding and pinching, playing emotion against emotion, and causing the general anxiety in the room to find inappropriate and reactive outlets in the form of accusations, innuendos, sarcasm, teasing, and hurtful tongue wagging. In no time at all the band of demons had managed to turn this oasis of Christian living into a whirlwind of anger, bitterness, and strife. In the end there was silence, but not a silence of peace. It was more like the silence after a battle, leaving in its wake only hurt feelings, rancor, and mistrust.

The team leader allowed his demonic gang of home wreckers to bask in the spoils of their petty and twisted victory for a few moments.

"All right you bunch of losers, let's go. We're done here!" he ordered. "This isn't the only stop tonight."

Hooting and howling, the demonic assault team piled into the ghost truck.

"Where to next, Boss?" asked Apagon with devilish glee in his squeaky voice.

"Hmm. Let's see," replied the team leader checking his clipboard. "Ah yes! You'll like this one . . . Next we go to Rev. Johnson's house. Ha! He thinks he's had a rough day. Wait till we get through with him!"

Scripture Study

- Luke 12:52, 53
- Proverbs 3:33; 11:28, 29; 19:13; 31:10-31
- Ephesians 6:10-17; 5:21-28
- Matthew 10:36-39

Study Questions

- Other than demons and devils, what else can explain anxious disharmony in a family?
- Is family disharmony caused primarily by external or internal forces? Explain.
- Are Christian families more immune to anxiety? Why or why not?
- Could the family in the story have taken measures to guard themselves from the results of their attack? How?

The Beach Ball

The beach was perfect. The sand was clean, the sea breeze was mild and sea-salty, and the ocean was calm and inviting. The cool lapping waves on the shore enticed many of the vacationers into the ocean.

On this sunny day the Gonzalez family ventured to the beach for a much-anticipated vacation. As soon as they arrived, Oliver, the oldest of the three children at five years of age, ran from the car peeling his clothes off as he headed straight for the water.

"Oliver! Wait for the rest of us," cried his mother, laughing at his enthusiasm.

But Oliver was already halfway to the shoreline carrying with him his newest favorite toy—a large, colorful beach ball more than half his size. The ball was huge. You couldn't help laughing as Oliver ran across the sand trying to balance the huge ball over his head.

Settling down on the large beach blanket, Oliver's father couldn't help but feel good; it was such a perfect day. The sun, the sea, the children happy and laughing, the homemade sandwiches and cold drinks, and of course the bright beach ball—all worked together to create the perfect holiday. "You can't ask for a better day," he thought to himself.

In the afternoon the warm breeze changed direction and started to blow toward the ocean. Prodded by the gentle breeze, the beach ball started slowly rolling toward the shoreline. Oliver went to retrieve the ball, but his small hands couldn't grasp the large ball. Every time he tried to get his short arms around the ball, it would pop away closer to the shore. As he chased the ball, Oliver got farther away from his family's spot on the beach and closer to the ocean.

"Oliver," his mother yelled after him, "come back!"

But Oliver saw only the ball. Even when he stepped into the ocean after the ball, Oliver did not hear his mother's yell, so focused was he at trying to retrieve his favorite toy. In the water the ball floated lightly on the surface. Every time Oliver's hand touched the light ball it would escape further away as if playing a game of tag.

"Oliver!" screamed his mother, standing on the edge of the ocean.

This time Oliver heard the urgency in his mother's voice and turned around. He was shocked to see how far he'd gone from the shore, and panicked when he realized that his feet did not touch the sandy ocean floor. Abandoning the ball, Oliver tried to turn back toward the beach. But he was too far into the ocean, and the light waves began to drag him further out.

Cold panic overtook him. He was not a swimmer, and so his violent thrashing only pulled him underwater. He was sinking and swallowing salt water—drowning! Terror seized Oliver as a cloud of darkness filled his mind and fear choked tight at his throat. Suddenly, however, he found himself in his father's arms, snatched from the sandy bottom. Scared but safe, he clung to his father as he was carried to shore and delivered to his mother's arms.

And what about the ball? It kept bobbing along the surface and moving toward the horizon, oblivious and uncaring as to its owner's plight.

Scripture Study

- Psalm 1
- Ephesians 6:1-6
- Proverbs 14:12; 16:25
- Colossians 4:14
- Genesis 12:10-20

Study Questions

- This story contains some allegorical components. What are they?
- Is sin an entity in and of itself, or is it a by-product of something else? Explain.
- Why is sin such an attractive force in our lives?
- Have you ever pursued a goal only to find yourself "drowning" because of it? Share your experience.

Like a Thief

As Peggy Innocenti answered the knock on her door, she muttered to herself, "Now who could that be at this hour?"

"Good evening, ma'am," said the stranger at the door. "Are you Mrs. Innocenti?"

"Good evening," replied Peggy, "Why, yes I am."

Despite being a young woman, she had become comfortable with the formal manner in which most people addressed her as "Mrs. Innocenti." Widowed five years, she enjoyed the status and respect that her former husband's small fortune provided. It had been a good marriage, though tragically cut short due to her husband's poor health. Some thought that Peggy made strategic use of her wealth, lands, and status to buffer some of the grieving pain she still carried.

"How can I help you?" she asked the man standing at her door.

"My name is Barrabas," said the man before her. "I am the executive director of an international organization of thieves and home burglars."

Indeed, Peggy had not failed to notice the man's unusual appearance, though she was much too polite to mention it. The man was wearing black slacks and a striped pullover shirt and sported a mask that covered his face from nose to brow. The eyes peeping through the mask's eyeholes were bright and animated.

"See here," cried Peggy sternly. "You leave this property right now, or I'll call the police!"

"Very well, ma'am," replied Barrabas calmly. "But you'll miss out on a great opportunity, and you'll give up a chance to win some fabulous prizes."

"Prizes?" asked Peggy, "What prizes?"

Well you see, Mrs. Innocenti," said Barrabas excitedly, "your house has been selected as the 'home of the month' in our home robber's association."

"Home of the month?" asked Peggy, her curiosity aroused, "Please, come in and tell me about it."

Barrabas entered the elegant foyer and closed the door behind him. He gave the adjacent rooms a quick but subtle "once over" with practiced eyes. As his eyes scanned the objects in the room—expensive antique furniture, works of art, Oriental rugs—another part of his brain was calculating their "resale" value.

"What did you say your name was?" asked Peggy.

"Barrabas, ma'am," said the thief, smiling and offering his hand. "Mr. Barrabas. You are a most fortunate woman, Mrs. Innocenti!" he exclaimed, motioning to the luxurious surroundings.

"Yes, I am fortunate," she said with aristocratic pride. "My husband left me a large fortune."

"No, no," responded the man, "I wasn't referring to your fortune. You are fortunate because you have been selected, out of hundreds of others I might add, to be robbed by our fine organization."

Not waiting for the puzzled and slightly shocked woman to answer, the thief hurriedly explained to her the privilege of the recognition and the benefits that accompanied the International Society of Thief and Home Burglar's "House of the Month" program. In addition to receiving fabulous prizes, the lucky owner of said house received an all-expense-paid trip to Hawaii, plus spending money and transportation to and from the airport.

The fast-talking Barrabas continued with his sales pitch. Peggy's excitement matched the rising pitch in the thief's voice until, without realizing it, she was giving him a tour of her fabulous house as he talked on and on. Soon she was pointing out her valued possessions, revealing the location of the hidden safe, highlighting the features of the security system, and noting which paintings were of worth and which were reproductions. By the time they found themselves back in the foyer of the house, the thief had produced a clipboard on which he had secured the signature of the excited owner.

"Very well, then," said the thief, double-checking his clipboard. "Next Friday at 3:00 PM we will be here to rob your house. Please remember to leave the door open and to disconnect the alarm before leaving."

"Yes, I'll remember," said Mrs. Innocenti, making a mental note.

"Our driver will be here that morning to take you to the airport," continued Barrabas. "Enjoy your trip!"

And sure enough, the following Friday morning a limousine and driver pulled up to the grand house of Mrs. Peggy Innocenti. As the limousine sped out of the driveway carrying a slightly excited but bemused Peggy, a half dozen vans and trucks pulled up to the front door of her house.

As promised, Mrs. Innocenti was delivered to the airport and escorted to a plane, which indeed headed to an island in the Pacific. Unfortunately for the naïve Peggy Innocenti, the island was not Hawaii but some smaller, nondescript, isolated island favored by merchant sailors, modern-day pirates, and other colorful though unsavory characters. There she was left stranded for the remainder of her days, a victim of her own greed and foolishness.

Scripture Study

- John 8:44; 10:30
- Matthew 10:16
- Colossians 4:5
- Revelation 16:15

Study Questions

- Have you ever "been taken for a ride," cheated, or scammed? Share your experience.
- Would you label most people as gullible? Why?
- In what ways do we allow ourselves to be "robbed blind" in the Christian life?
- Does greed make us vulnerable? If so, how?

Peter and the Shadow

Peter was a bad man, a very bad man. In his lifetime he had committed countless delinquencies, crimes, and sins. In fact, his wickedness and violent behavior had earned him a respectable reputation in the underworld of crime and corruption. His criminal reputation coupled with his uncanny ability to escape capture and punishment from the legal system earned him two nicknames: "Lucky" and "The Reprobate." The first nickname some of his more intimate associates would call him to his face; the latter was uttered only behind his back.

In contrast to the usual notions of the sad fate of the criminal class, Lucky lived well. He enjoyed a lifestyle most would envy: money, possessions, women, power. He had it all and then some, including good looks and a natural cunning that kept him two steps ahead of the law. To all who knew him or knew of him, Peter was "untouchable."

Sometimes God is patient, seemingly allowing evil to have its way. Then good persons ask, "Why do the evil prosper?" But however mysterious God's ways and timing remain to finite minds, God does act. One fateful day Lucky caught God's attention. And that was the day Lucky's luck ran out, because on that day God sent a blob of a shadow to follow that infamous scoundrel.

The shadow was no more than a small shapeless blob attached to Lucky's feet. Other than being a curiosity, he paid little attention to it at first. But with each crime committed, with each willful act of sin, with each intentional act of violence Peter committed, the shadow grew and took form. Soon Peter noted that the shadow was darker and blacker than the shadow produced by any earthly object. The way the shadow seemed to absorb light and move on its own became unsettling not only to the sinner attached to it, but also to all those around him. Soon, Peter found himself alone more often as people avoided being around him and his shadow.

Growing more and more anxious in the relentless presence of the living shadow, Peter tried to numb himself with drugs and alcohol. But the shadow seemed to have the power to absorb the intoxicating effects of those substances. So Peter was left alert to the constant companionship of that abyss of darkness.

As Peter continued in his loathsome ways, sin upon sin fed the shadow, and it became darker, bigger, and colder. Until one day, the miserable man noticed that the shadow had grown big enough to fill any room he entered. No amount of light in the room would diminish the shadow. No heating unit was able to raise the room temperature above a chill when Peter entered a room followed by the shadow. Now the constant swaying and fluid convolutions of his dark companion became so unsettling as to be maddening.

Then one fateful day Peter was sitting alone and desperate in a corner of his room where a single ray of sunlight managed to push its way through the thickness of the shadow that filled the room from top to bottom. Suddenly, something new and terrible happened. The shadow seemed to sprout two huge arms, cold and physical, that reached slowly but relentlessly toward Peter's throat.

Unable to move as he witnessed this horror, Peter sat watching wide-eyed as the bodily shadow-arms spread dark icy fingers across his chest and coiled around his throat. At the last moment before losing consciousness, Peter, who long ago ceased to be called Lucky by his friends and acquaintances, tore himself from the deadly grip of the shadow and ran out of his house. He ran through the streets screaming until he reached a police station. Reaching the front desk, he screamed, "Help me! Help me! It's after me! It's trying to kill me!"

As some police officers tried to get the raving man under control, others ran into the street to try to find whoever was terrorizing him. These returned shortly, not having found anything or anyone suspicious outside.

They looked to the trembling man and asked, "Who's trying to kill you? There's no one out there."

"The shadow!" cried Peter. "It's the shadow. It's chasing me, trying to kill me. Please help me! Keep it away! The shadow!"

One officer looked at the trembling man and said, "Hey, isn't that Lucky Peter?"

The other officers recognized the man as the notorious criminal who had escaped them for so long. Giving each other a knowing look, they grabbed the poor man and threw him out into the street.

"No, please, no!" cried the desperate Peter. "Throw me in jail! Please lock me up! Don't set me free!"

Turning away from the precinct door that slammed in his face, Peter glanced nervously behind him. The shadow had not followed him into the precinct, so no one inside had seen the phenomenal and terrible shadow of Peter's living nightmare. But there was the shadow, waiting for him in the light of the day, leaving a long, black cold smear across the street.

With a desperate and hopeless chill in his heart, Peter turned and ran down the street, turning corner after corner. Glancing back in terror, he saw the shadow's relentless pursuit bringing it closer and closer. And that is the last anyone saw of "Lucky" Peter, running and screaming down the city streets, fleeing, with all his sins in pursuit.

Scripture Study

- Luke 12:2, 3
- 1 Corinthians 4:4, 5
- Hebrews 12:1, 2
- 2 Samuel 12:5-7
- Joshua 7:18-26

Study Questions

- Is guilt a good or a bad thing? Why?
- Will evil persons reap a just reward in their lives? Why or why not?
- To what extent does God intervene directly in people's lives? Explain.
- Is it possible for persons to "sear" their conscience so that they feel no guilt for their sin?

Don't Get
Your Wires Crossed

It used to be that demented or misguided people were said to have their "wires crossed." That's because their behavior often seemed misguided and misinformed. That phrase, "He must have his wires crossed," isn't used often today, but it reminds me of a man who once decided to save money by performing the car maintenance on his vehicle himself. He figured he'd save a lot of money by changing the oil, performing a tune-up, and replacing the spark plugs and air filter. Basic auto care—"How difficult could it be?" he asked himself.

So one weekend he bought the parts, took out his tools, and spent the day working on (and on occasion swearing at) his car in the driveway as his wife kept him supplied with iced tea. As she walked back to the house, she would shake her head and sympathetically think, "Men! Who can understand them?" After bringing out the second tray of iced tea she decided it wasn't a good idea to ask, "How's it going, Honey?" It took all day, longer than he had anticipated such simple jobs would. But at the end of the day he was a satisfied man with a gratifying sense of accomplishment. Five times that evening he'd say to his wife, "You know how much I saved by doing all that myself?"

"No," she'd lovingly reply each time. "How much exactly?"

"Well, I don't know exactly," he'd say, "But it was a *lot* I can tell you that!" And he'd smile a satisfied smile as he looked out at his car in the driveway.

But two days later the car began to act up, lurching, hesitating, and giving out loud knocks and pings from under the hood. After that the car would unpredictably decelerate even with one's foot on the gas pedal. Then after four days the car would lurch forward and stall when the man stepped on the gas at a light.

After a couple of days of being late to every appointment and wondering if he'd get home at the end of the day, the man was stressed and frustrated. Other drivers were honking their horns at him and giving him mean looks. Worse, every kind of car was passing him on the road, leaving him perpetually watching a stream of receding tail lights. After his second close call narrowly avoiding an accident because of the car's erratic behavior, the man became a nervous wreck.

The pride he had felt in his handiwork was forgotten. Now he feared that to fix all the problems he was having with his car would cost him hundreds of dollars—money he didn't have. But by the end of the week the car was in such a sad state that he had no choice. He swallowed his pride, braced himself for the inevitable costly repair bill, and took his car to his auto mechanic. The man didn't know what he feared most—having to pay a bill he really could not afford, or confessing to his mechanic that he had tried to fix the car himself, resulting in this tragic and embarrassing situation.

Standing with his cap in his hand, the man watched as his mechanic poked his head under the hood. The experienced mechanic looked all of two minutes and then said, "I see what the problem is. Look here," he pointed, "you've got your wires crossed!"

The mechanic pulled out two wires, examined the ends briefly, then crossed them and plugged them back into their right places. The motor sprang to life and hummed like a kitten.

"That's it?" cried the man.

"That's it," said the mechanic, grinning.

"Umm. How much?" asked the man.

"Nothing," replied the mechanic. "Next time just bring it in, okay?"

The man drove his car though the streets, humming along. He took the highway home, racing the engine and enjoying the smooth quiet ride. It felt like a new car! No one could imagine that just an hour ago this same car was stalling and lurching and coughing its way along. There never was anything really wrong with the engine. It just had its wires crossed, which prevented the engine from getting the power it needed to do its work. Needless to say, the lesson was not lost on the man. Humbly he realized that this wouldn't have happened if he had not tried to be something he was not. In his eagerness to save money and boast of his expertise, he had gotten the wires crossed.

Scripture Study

- Hebrews 12:1,2; 4:14-16
- Acts 1:8, 18-22
- John 12:4-8
- Matthew 17:18-21
- James 4:3-6

Study Questions

- Can you provide a "spiritual moral" to this story?
- Have you ever learned a lesson the hard way? Share your experience.
- Are most lessons in the Christian life learned the hard way? Why or why not?
- Other than the hard way, what other ways are there to learn about the Christian life?

You Reap What You Sow

This is the story of Clement and his good neighbor, Ambrose. They were farmers who toiled and teased the soil to feed their families and to provide for the needs of their small community. Despite their hard work, there was never enough money for the ever-growing needs of their families, much less money left over for needed improvements on their farms. Money was so scarce that neither could recall the last time they had even thought of investing. Theirs was the hard day-to-day existence of the simple people of the land.

One day, however, their fortunes changed. Working at mending the fence that separated their adjacent farmland, they uncovered some buried treasure. Because they had found the treasure on both their lands (technically), and being good neighbors who had long shared their resources and plight, they agreed that the money belonged equally to both of them. Filled with joy at this change of fortune, they decided to go to town to buy seed and fertilizer to increase their crop. They calculated that with the seed they would buy and the increased yield in the harvest, the winter would be less harsh, and the promise of a better life was just within reach.

They hitched the old mule to the wagon and prepared to head for town to invest their newfound fortune. Being habitually frugal, Clement and Ambrose wanted to get as much seed as they could afford. Rather than pay for new sacks, they decided that they would save money by using their own sacks to carry the seed rather than pay extra for new sacks. So they hunted around and found some old, worn and torn sacks. They hastily mended any holes they found in the sack, then threw them in back of the wagon and headed for town.

On their return trip from town they were so happy, they did not notice that as the wagon jostled and jumped along the road it loosened the hastily stitched holes in their torn sacks. Before long the seed on which they had put their hopes for a better life was pouring out of the sacks and onto the road. The old sacks containing the rich fertilizer also ripped open. Like sand from an hourglass, the rich substance trickled off the wagon and into the ruts left by the wagon wheels. As Clement and Ambrose dreamed privately of their eventual affluence, seed and fertilizer mixed in the furrowed ruts on the road they unknowingly plowed and sowed. By the time they arrived home, the torn sacks had spilled almost all of the planting seed and fertilizer, and along with them, all of their hopes.

They stood staring at the torn sacks, embarrassed and embittered for their frugality. Then with sadness and resignation, without a word, each turned to his own home, both leaving their dreams of an easier life on the road behind them. That night the change of season brought the rains that signaled an end to the planting season. And with the rain came thoughts of regret and despair as Clement and Ambrose contemplated the fate of their families at the end of a year without a harvest. Surely they would starve.

As the weeks passed, Clement and Ambrose suffered silently through their despair. With little to do but wait for nothing, they became recluses on their farms, going through the motions of performing mundane chores that at least provided the numbness of routine. When harvest time came, so did their darkest hour as they stared at the meager yield of their fields. There was barely enough to feed their families and certainly not enough to barter into enough money for another planting. The two friends despaired of all hope.

But then something amazing happened. Two weeks after the harvest time, neighbors from the surrounding community began to arrive one after another with gifts for Clement and Ambrose and their families. Many brought food and clothing. Some brought materials and housewares. Others brought seed for the next planting. The outpouring of neighborly generosity was appreciated and overwhelming. The gifts kept coming as almost every member of the community dropped by bringing not only a package, but also words of thanks.

It seems that the seed that had spilled out of the torn sacks onto the roads (along with Clement and Ambrose's hopes) grew and flourished during their long months of despair. The once barren and little-traveled roads of that small community became a rich field of harvest. Neighbors from all over harvested and gleaned the bounty. The grain became a lifesaver for the other poor farm families in the community. They made bread and ate as much as they wanted, then sold the rest of the grain in the market. Following the narrow and golden harvest road straight to the farms of Clement and Ambrose, they were able to discover who their benefactors were. Clement and Ambrose had sown, and the community reaped, and now they all shared in the bounty. At the end of their time of despair and hopelessness, Clement and Ambrose saw their treasure multiply and their families saved for a future brighter than they could have imagined.

Scripture Study

- Jeremiah 18:1-6
- Isaiah 53:10-12
- 1 Corinthians 3:6-9
- Genesis 12:1-3
- 1 Peter 2:9-11

Study Questions

- Have you ever come across unexpected treasure or experienced a financial windfall? Share your experience.
- Have you ever experienced a misfortune or disaster that in the end turned out to be a blessing? Share your experience.
- Has someone shared with you that you were a blessing in his or her life? How did that make you feel? What did that mean to you?
- Have you ever been the recipient of someone else's generosity and kindness? How did that make you feel? What did that mean to you?

The Wall

Once upon a time there was a great kingdom, filled with peace and prosperity. Actually, this fabled realm was made up of two neighboring kingdoms: the Blue and the Green. They lived together as harmonious as the sea with the sky. In fact, so agreeable was the relationship between the Blue kingdom and the Green kingdom that people referred to them together as the Land of Bluegreen.

Just one king ruled this twin kingdom. The king sat on the throne in his palace in the Blue country, but every day he would walk among his subjects of the Green country. He was a just king, treating all his subjects with equal respect, compassion, and severity as the occasion called for. He had won the hearts of his subjects, so there was harmony in the kingdom.

One day, however, one of the young princes of the Blue realm rebelled against the benevolent and beloved king. In a tragic and misguided battle he led an unsuccessful attempt to overthrow the king. Many lives were lost, and many more hearts were broken to see shattered the fabled harmony that the Land of Bluegreen had enjoyed for ages. Defeated, the rebel prince and his many followers were cast out of the Blue kingdom.

The bitter young prince went into exile in the Green kingdom. Soon, with great cunning he managed to incite a great part of the population to rebel against the neighboring Blue kingdom and its king. As a result of the sporadic fighting and the threat of further conflict, a large wall was constructed to divide the two kingdoms. The Blue kingdom with the king was on one side of the wall, and the Green kingdom with the rebellious prince was on the other. And so ended the fabled Land of Bluegreen.

As the people in the Green kingdom became more and more alienated from the king and his subjects, the wall that divided the kingdoms rose higher and higher. Only one man from the Green kingdom remained in the land of the Blue. He had remained loyal to the king. For years the man tried to win the subjects of his home country back to the realm of the good king. Daily he would stand by the only small door on the vast wall that separated the kingdoms. This door was the only way into the Blue kingdom, and one reached it only after a difficult and perilous journey. Those who sought the door and heeded the words of the faithful servant of the king were welcomed into the Blue kingdom and lived in harmony with their brethren again.

But the great majority of the citizens in the Green kingdom remained rebellious. In their zeal to remain separate from the king and his subjects, they continued to build the wall higher and higher. Dismayed, the king sent messengers to the Green kingdom with an offer of reconciliation and peace for any who would join the citizens in the Blue kingdom. But so alienated were the Green citizens that they beat and imprisoned the king's messengers. And with each brutal act, the wall grew higher and higher.

Soon the wall was so high that the Green kingdom was in perpetual gloom because neither the light of the sun nor the glow of harmony and goodness from the Blue kingdom could rise above the wall of hate that separated the cities. The citizens of the Green kingdom added daily to the wall, so every day it grew higher. Soon the separation was complete so that even the small door through which many had passed to find peace and forgiveness was forgotten. It became overgrown with weeds and vines. Eventually the rust of neglect froze the lock and hinges, and the door remained shut for four hundred years. No longer did the king's messengers venture into the Green kingdom with their message of reconciliation and forgiveness. As the years passed, it was not only an insurmountable wall that separated the kingdoms, but also a hopeless silence.

Then one day the old rusty door creaked open. Through it passed a young lamb from the Blue kingdom. This lamb had the power to heal sicknesses, perform signs, and win the hearts of people to embrace peace. Many were blessed by the lamb, and he brought healing to those who were ill of spirit, mind, and body. But when the people of the Green land discovered that the lamb had come from the land of Blue, they hunted him down.

Filled with their long-held hatred for the king, the people of the Green land persecuted and mistreated the lamb, despite all of the good he had done for them. So deep was their animosity that in their fury they dragged the peaceful creature to the wall that bordered the kingdom and nailed him to it by his hoofs. There they taunted and tortured the submissive lamb, cursing the king who had sent him. As the cruelty of the mob escalated, the darkness that hung over the land of Green grew deeper until the sun was completely blocked from the

sky. In that hour total darkness ruled over the land *and* the hearts of
the citizens of the Green kingdom; and it is said that in that hour, the
wall of separation grew to its highest point.

Then, at the exact moment that the wall and the darkness
reached the apex of their intensity, something amazing happened. As
the blood from the dying lamb trickled down the wall of separation,
small cracks and fissures began to appear. The cracks along the wall
followed the tracks of blood seeping from the lamb, and as the cracks
widened, rays of light from the Blue kingdom streamed into the darkness of the Green kingdom, slicing through the oppression that
covered the land as thick as tar.

As the blood continued to flow down the wall, its redemptive
power breached the enormous structure, shaking it from the ground
up to its unassailable height. When the wall could not support its own
weight at the point where the blood ate away at decades of alienation
and separation, it collapsed, crashing down upon the lamb and bury-
ing it under a mountain of rubble. The lamb disappeared, entombed
under the debris of the crumbled wall. For three days the wall continued to fall. The king and his subjects in the Blue kingdom cried
and wailed as they watched the wall continue to bury the beloved
lamb. Their hearts broke as they lost all hope of ever rescuing it. But
in the land the Green the people gloated over their self-proclaimed
victory.

For three days the wall crumbled, and as more light streamed into
the Green kingdom, its evil citizens fled further into the darker cor-
ners of their land. And then something even more amazing happened.
The giant pile of stones that had become the tomb for the lamb
exploded upward like lava spewed from an angry volcano. The power
of the explosion threw debris for miles into the sky and through the
land, and smoke and fire blazed at the center of the explosion. When
the fire died down and the smoke cleared, those who had dared to
remain witnessed an awesome spectacle. For a moment the lamb
stood amid the rubble under the breach in the wall, radiant and white
like no other lamb. And then an amazing transformation took place.
The lamb changed shape: its head turned into that of a lion, and its
body became a golden gate that filled the breach on the wall.

From that day on, the lamb of the king became the guardian of
the only opening between the two kingdoms, standing on the spot
where he had sacrificed his life and where his blood had burned a hole
in the wall of separation. Whenever someone from the Green kingdom would approach the gate humbly and with repentance, the lamb

with the face of a lion and the body of a golden gate opened its doors and let the person pass into the Blue kingdom of light and harmony. But all others he kept at bay with a terrible roar and barred gates that no one could breach.

The king, too, welcomed all from the Green kingdom who fled the darkness that remained in that hopeless land. But he looked forward to the day when the whole wall of separation would come tumbling down. For on that day the lamb would return to sit at his right hand, and the light of the Blue kingdom would flood the entire land. On that day people would once again call his kingdom the Bluegreen, for he would again rule over all of his subjects in peace and harmony.

Scripture Study

- Genesis 3:9; 6:8, 14-22
- Ezekiel 28:11-19
- Isaiah 14:12-17; 59:1-2
- Revelation 5:5, 6; 12:7-9; 19:11-16
- John 1:29; 14:6
- Matthew 5:12

Study Questions

- This story contains several allegorical elements. What are they? What do they represent?
- Do Christians hold "dual citizenship" in this world and the next, or are they citizens of only one realm? Explain.
- Have you ever experienced a wall of separation between yourself and God? What made the wall crumble?
- Why do some people seem so resistant to the good news of God's provision for redemption?

Advice from the Night Visitors

A certain Christian named Lloron found himself in an unfortunate season of his life, afflicted by diverse problems and trials. Day after day his situation got worse, his problems multiplying. The more he tried to fix matters, the worse they got.

In the midst of his desperation he prayed to God, asking for help. Despite his fervent prayers, only silence came as a reply. Feeling abandoned by God during his time of greatest need, one evening he fell asleep hopeless and weeping.

In the middle of the night he dreamed a strange dream, one unlike any before. He saw himself standing on a beach, facing the ocean, dark and forbidding. Suddenly, a great fish rose from the depths, its enormous mouth opening wider as it approached the shore. The monster lunged toward him, its giant head towering over him, and its cavernous mouth looking like it would swallow him whole. Instead, the great fish regurgitated a horrible figure of a man; and as suddenly as it appeared, the great fish was swallowed by the ocean.

The strange man before Lloron struggled to his feet, his weak legs struggling to find balance on the sand. Turning toward Lloron, he said, "Peace to you. My name is Jonah, and I have been sent to give you some advice."

Lloron looked at the specter before him in shock, for the man was a horror to behold. Besides his repulsive stench, the man's matted and singed hair, mottled skin, and emaciated torso made him look like an emissary from the undead.

Without waiting for a reply and dismissing the obvious look of horror on the face of Lloron, the man continued, "My advice to persons with problems like yours is simple: You must flee from your problems."

"Flee?" stammered Lloron in reply.

"Yes, flee. Run away!" answered Jonah. "Not that running away will solve your problems in the end."

The man who called himself Jonah proceeded to tell his tale of how he had run from God and his dilemma.

"You saw the fish," he continued. "That cursed great fish was sent by God to keep me in its belly for three days. I ran away from my problem only to encounter a larger one. Run away from your problems, Lloron. That is my advice."

With those last words Jonah turned toward the sea and disappeared like a ghost in the mist of the ocean spray. Lloron tossed in his sleep, recalling in his dreams all the times he had run away from his problems and from God, the only one who could have helped him. He realized that he had learned this supposed solution from his father, a man who when confronted with any difficulty would seek solace and escape in a bottle of liquor. The greater the problem, the more he would try to drown it in drink. But like Jonah, he could not drown his problems; instead, they drowned him.

"Good evening," a new voice in his dream greeted.

"And who are you?" asked Lloron, beginning to get accustomed to the misty world of this strange dream.

"My name is Job, and I have been sent to give you some advice," answered the man, ancient-looking and covered with boils. A look of utter loss and raw grief colored his eyes.

"More advice?" pondered Lloron.

"So it is," answered the ancient one.

"Will you tell me to run away, too?" asked Lloron.

"No," replied Job. "My advice to you is to be resigned to your fate. Only then will you manage to survive your despair."

"Has that served you well?" asked Lloron.

"Up to a point," responded Job. "I have not denied God in the midst of my trials, and I have not run away from my problems, choosing instead to resign myself to my fate. But in being resigned to the circumstances in my life, I gave birth within me to profound bitterness and depression."

"In other words," replied Lloron, "your advice won't help me, will it?"

"My advice will serve you well. But you may need something else," replied Job's fading voice as the old man faded like a distant memory before Lloron.

"Wait! Don't go yet!" cried Lloron, surprising himself. Why would he want that miserable man's company, he wondered. Finally he murmured to himself, "Misery loves company, I guess."

Lloron tossed about in his sleep again, kicking the blankets off the bed. But even the chill in the air could not awaken him from this mysterious dream. In his dream he found himself on the outskirts of a dusty ancient city. A crowd streamed from the nearest gate, forming a procession that followed a familiar-looking man. Hunched under a heavy burden, the sad figure labored to make his way to a hill beyond the walled city.

"Why doesn't anyone help him?" wondered Lloron to himself.

The man and his entourage made their way toward Lloron. As the man with the burden on his back neared Lloron, he could see that the man's body was battered and bloody. The sweat from his body pooled beneath his feet, causing him to slip and stumble on the rocks along the unpaved road. Lloron was certain that he knew this man, but try as he might he could not remember—the hazy realm of dreams did not allow him to recall a name or a meeting or the context of a memory where he had met this sad man.

As the man was passing him by, Lloron called out, "Wait. Do you have something for me?"

The man paused in front of Lloron. Up close he seemed a more tragic figure than the two previous visitors in his dream, yet there was something different about this one.

"Yes, I have something for you," replied the man with the burden.

"Do you have some advice for me?" asked Lloron, disregarding the crowd that was beginning to gather behind this man they were following.

"Yes, I have been sent to give you some advice—this is the third and final one you will receive," replied the man with a voice of strength and conviction despite his heartbreaking appearance.

"And what is your advice?" asked Lloron.

"Give me the burden of your problems, trials, worries, and anxieties," replied the man. "Put them here on my back, and I will carry your burdens for you."

"But sir," replied Lloron, "you are already carrying the weight of the world on your back. How can you take mine, too?"

"I can bear your burdens," replied the man. "That is what I have been sent to tell you. My advice to you is this: give me your burdens, and I will give you courage to go on."

Moved to tears, Lloron stood before the man, overwhelmed with a feeling of peace and relief. Suddenly, he awoke from his dream with the light of the sun falling on his face. His mind tried to retain the fading dream that was now slipping from his consciousness in the light of day.

Scripture Study

- Psalm 81:1-7
- Matthew 11:29-30
- Isaiah 53:11
- Romans 15:1
- Galatians 6:2

Study Questions

- What is the best advice you've ever received? Did you follow it?
- What is meant by the idea that Jesus "bears our burdens"?
- Has someone shared your burden? What did that mean to you? What did it feel like?
- Are there some burdens that cannot be shared with others? Are there some burdens that cannot be shared with God?

The Cloth

Sebastian was the world's best tailor. His formal suits and evening gowns could be seen hanging in the wardrobes of royalty and celebrities throughout the world. Kings and queens, princes and princesses, courtiers and the rich and powerful vied for Sebastian's first creations of each new fashion season. Movie stars were known to forego galas and award shows because they had been unable to obtain one of Sebastian's creations to wear to the occasion.

Indeed, Sebastian was a true genius in his field. He could create the most appealing clothing out of the most common materials. There was no style, popular or extravagant, he could not create. He could satisfy those with the most eccentric taste in couture. And he could meet the challenge of even the most outrageous of celebrities in their quest for vanity and attention. He was, in effect, an artist.

One day a package arrived at Sebastian's studio. It contained a new type of cloth from the Orient—a mysterious and magnificent piece, colorful, rich in texture. It was a delight to the eye and touch. Every customer who saw it wanted an article of clothing made out of the new shimmering fabric. But Sebastian had only enough cloth for one outfit at best. Who would he choose to receive an outfit made out of the extravagant and mysterious cloth?

But Sebastian's greatest dilemma turned out not to be a matter of deciding who would be the lucky recipient of a new magnificent outfit—a matter that could have dire consequences given the nature of his clientele—but the cloth itself. As it happens, the cloth was from an exotic land in the Orient where cloth is not cut or sown to make clothing. As was their custom for ages, the people of that land merely wrapped the long cloth around their bodies in a uniquely fashionable way, leaving the cloth intact.

When the mysterious cloth saw Sebastian the tailor coming after it with a pair of scissors, it ran away in horror. What was that man trying to do to it? Was he trying to mutilate its beautiful pattern by cutting it apart like the other rags he had seen him working with? For three days the cloth managed to keep out of the reach of the master tailor.

Finally, with the help of his assistant, Sebastian managed to capture the mysterious cloth. They wrestled it to their worktable where they pinned it down flat. As the terrified cloth watched, they layed a pattern over it and commenced to outline the different parts of a suit. Soon, Sebastian was cutting strips off the cloth in the shapes he would need: collar, pockets, lapels, back panel, sleeves, and vest. All the while the cloth was screaming in horror. When Sebastian the tailor was done, the only part left of the cloth was a pile of strips. The cloth was horrified at this insanity. What had this madman done? He had mutilated a beautiful and perfect piece of cloth and left a jumble of useless strips all over the table.

To make matters worse, the tailor gathered the assorted cut pieces and placed them in a dark drawer where it lay for days. Apparently forgotten, the cloth sat in darkness and misery, aghast at the fate that had befallen it. "I am now just a worthless rag," lamented the cloth.

But Sebastian had not forgotten the cloth. All the time the cloth lay in despair, the master tailor was thinking and planning as to what he would create out of the cloth, and about who would be the recipient of the masterpiece he hoped to create. Finally, sufficiently inspired, Sebastian retrieved the cloth from the drawer. Finding itself on the worktable again, the cloth began to moan and whine.

"Stop crying!" cried Sebastian. "I cannot work with you whining like that."

Armed with needle and thread, the master tailor began to sew the pieces of cloth together. Each stitch pinched the cloth, and as the thread ran through its rich body, it felt constricted and thought it would choke. The more Sebastian worked at his masterpiece, the more miserable felt the cloth, for while the master tailor envisioned his final masterpiece, the cloth only experienced the pain and discomfort of the moment.

Sebastian stitched here, cut there, tucked here, stretched there, for the most part not paying attention to the cries from the miserable cloth. Every once in a while the cloth would let out a loud squeak when the sewing needle pinched it. On those occasions the annoyed tailor would snap, "Be still you worthless piece of cloth!" And that would hurt more than any needle pinch could.

The master tailor worked for three days. And for three days the cloth lived a most miserable existence, experiencing a fate no cloth from his home country could ever imagine: to be cut to pieces and then to be stitched back together, seamed with scars throughout its once-perfect form. But on the fourth day Sebastian the tailor finished his work, and the cloth's torture was over.

Sebastian hung the finished outfit before a mirror to admire it— and the cloth was astounded beyond belief. In the reflection he saw himself as never before—a magnificent tailored outfit unlike any other in the world. Indeed, it was a masterpiece! Then, looking at Sebastian the tailor, it saw reflected in the eyes of its maker all the pride and love that went into its creation. For the first time it noticed the tailor's bleeding fingers, the weary brow and hunched shoulders from sleepless nights and countless hours of work. But it was the look of admiration that held its gaze, for at that moment it realized that it was not out of malice that the tailor had inflicted so much pain, but out of a desire to shape it by design into the magnificent outfit he had envisioned in his mind.

The next day Sebastian lovingly wrapped the suit and placed it in an ornate gift box. This he carried to the palace of the most noble king he knew, the only one of his clients who had not asked for the cloth out of vain motives. He presented the suit to the good king who wore it with pride and lovingly cared for it all his days.

Scripture Study

- Isaiah 64:6
- Philippians 1:6
- Ephesians 4:13
- Jeremiah 18:1-6
- John 15:1-5

Study Questions

- Is it easy or difficult for Christians to give themselves over completely to being shaped by God? Why?
- Why do significant growth and learning often require pain?
- Did you ever experience a difficult time in your life when you could not understand how God was present? Share your experience.
- Does God intentionally allow pain to enable growth and a greater good to come of it? Why? Can you give a biblical example? Can you give an example from your life experience?

Abel and His Lamp

Abel was twelve years old and on the adventure of a lifetime. His parents took him on a vacation trip to the Orient! Their itinerary included Israel, Egypt, Iran, Turkey, and various Arabian countries. Usually, their travel and sightseeing were dictated by the usual tours given to groups and spectator visitors. But in some places, family friends gave them a more intimate introduction to the lands and the people. These were by far Abel's favorite excursions, for he appreciated that he was able to see places and experience things the usual visitor did not.

One afternoon the family toured an ancient mountain fortress in the isolated outskirts of an Arab country. This ancient spot was not part of any regular tour; it was of more interest to historians and archaeologists. A good friend of Abel's father had taken them there to spend a leisurely afternoon away from the crowded city. After a long lunch Abel was allowed to go exploring on his own, since the guide had assured his parents that it was safe to do so. Abel wandered through ancient ruins, hilltops and valleys, and a dusty wadi that he knew would carry a torrential river when the rainy season hit the distant mountains.

All of a sudden Abel came upon a cave opening at the base of an ancient wall set into a cliff face. Being more curious than brave, he could not resist the temptation to explore the dark recesses of the cave. Of course, his young mind was full of images of buried treasure—gold, rubies, and precious stones. But he knew that was just wishful thinking and a little boy's imagination. Just as he was about to return to the mouth of the cave, the light from his flashlight reflected off of something dull but metallic. He squeezed further into the cave and pulled out a half-buried small wooden chest. It was about the size of a shoebox and sealed with two iron bands. Excited, Abel put the box in his backpack and headed back to the camp.

Upon arriving at the camp he found his parents hurriedly packing. They wanted to get home before dark, so they immediately instructed Abel to help with the packing. There was a lot of packing to do before leaving, and soon Abel forgot about his find that was tucked away in his backpack.

About a week later, after the family was home from vacation, Abel remembered the small box and hunted for it in his messy room. Eventually, he found it under a pile of dirty clothing, climbing equip‐ ment, rollerblades, and last year's returned homework assignments. (Abel's parents had long since stopped trying to get him to keep his room clean. Despite their dismay at the clutter and mess, they decided they had other more important issues to worry about than their son's dirty room. After all, he had to live in it, not they. And they were grateful for that at least!)

Abel labored for hours to open the ancient box. The more he worked at trying to pry it open, the more mysterious it seemed. It was as if it was guarding some ancient treasure or deep secret. Finally, with a pop and a swoosh of air, the box opened, spraying a cloud of dust around the room. Abel looked inside, and his jaw dropped. There, nestled at the bottom of the box was an ancient oil lamp—just like the one in the story of Aladdin. Could it be a "magic" lamp? Could such things really exist?

Abel carefully took the lamp out of its box and held it gingerly in his hands. He knew what he wanted to do, but it was a long time before he dared to rub the lamp. Finally, he gathered enough courage to hold the ancient brass lamp tightly in one hand while he rubbed frantically with the other. He rubbed and rubbed until he could feel the heat from the friction on his sweaty palm. There appeared a shiny spot where his hand had rubbed countless years of grime from the metal surface.

No genie appeared from the lamp, despite Abel's enthusiastic rubbing and wishful thinking. But just when he was about to give up and toss the lamp aside like some curious but worthless artifact, some‐ thing amazing happened. Beginning with a dull, throbbing glint the color of copper, a light grew brighter and brighter until it became a blinding flash that flooded the room like an exploding nova. The strange light was blinding, but it gave out no heat.

When Abel's eyes were able to adjust to the gloom of daylight flooding in through the windows of his room (the flash of light was a thousand times brighter than sunlight), he could hardly believe what he saw. The light from the lamp had cleaned every inch of his messy room! Not only was the room spotless, but everything was neatly in place. Clothes were clean and hung in the closet. Toys were shelved. Books were organized. Magazines were stacked. Papers were filed.

Trash was in the wastebasket. And the desktop that had not seen the light of day for months was cleared, organized, and orderly.

But not only was the room clean; Abel stood smiling from ear to ear, because he felt clean both inside and outside. The power of the lamp was not to grant wishes, but to clean anything in the path of its pure light.

Just then Abel's mother and father appeared at the door, saying, "Abel! Don't forget to clean your . . ."

They stopped mid-sentence, astounded at a sight they'd never seen before: Abel's room was spotless!

"How did you . . ." mumbled Abel's father.

"Oh my!" exclaimed his mother. "How wonderful! How did you do this?"

"It's the lamp," said Abel, still shocked from the experience of the purifying lamp. "It's a magic lamp. I rubbed it, and it cleaned my room."

Abel's parents looked at each other, then laughed aloud.

"Sure, Abel," replied his father. "And did the genie give you two more wishes? Ha, ha!"

"Oh, Abel," laughed his mother, "You've got such an imagination. But good work cleaning your room. We're proud of you."

Abel's parents closed the door behind them as they walked away, laughing at the thought of a magic lamp cleaning their son's messy room.

Abel was hurt and confused that his parents would not believe that the lamp had the power to clean his room. And he was sad that they would not feel the same joy he felt when the light of the lamp covered him with its cleansing light. From that day on, Abel kept the power of the lamp a secret. Every night he took the lamp out of its ancient wooden box, called forth its cleansing light, and basked in the joy and feeling of peace and cleanliness it gave. But he never shared the magic of the lamp with his parents, friends, or anyone he met his entire life.

Scripture Study

- John 8:12
- Matthew 5:14-16
- Matthew 28:18-20
- Luke 15:1-10

Study Questions

- Have you ever discovered something that totally changed your life? What was it? Describe how your life changed.
- There are some allegorical components to this story. What are they? What do they represent?
- Have you ever possessed something—an object, an idea, a truth, a piece of information—that you kept to yourself even though you knew someone might benefit from it? Share your experience.
- Do most Christians openly and willingly share the good news they possess? Why or why not?

New Shoes

"Pastor, I want a divorce!"

It was Wednesday evening just after the midweek prayer meeting at Benton Community Church. Josh Browning, the senior pastor, was taken by surprise by this unexpected (and fervent) announcement. For the moment all he managed to say was, "Why?"

"Because I can't take it anymore! I'm sick and tired of this relationship," replied the parishioner.

"But didn't I marry you and your spouse about three months ago?"

"Ten weeks and three days," fumed the angry church member.

"And you want out already?" asked Pastor Browning, leading the way to his study.

"Yes. I'm uncomfortable and irritated all the time. I feel stifled and trapped. I feel like I don't have room to breathe."

"I see," replied the pastor. "Before you make any hasty decisions, allow me to tell you a story."

Too confused and angry to reply, the parishioner plopped down on a chair as Pastor Browning began telling his story.

"Once upon a time there was a young woman engaged to a wonderful young man. The wedding day was drawing closer, and everything was ready. The church, the minister, the banquet, the beautiful wedding gown, everything except for . . . the wedding shoes. Even though the bride had ordered the shoes months ago, they were the only thing yet to arrive.

"Finally, the new wedding shoes arrived on her wedding day. It was a beautiful pair of white shoes, imported from France, especially handcrafted for the bride. What a relief she felt when the shoes arrived at the last minute! She was ready to get married! The bride put on the brand new shoes and headed for the Rolls Royce limousine that would take her to the church and her patiently waiting husband-to-be.

"At first the shoes felt a little bit tight, but they looked so nice on her that she didn't mind a little discomfort. The shoemaker had promised, 'The more you wear them, the better they get.'

"She arrived at the church and walked down the aisle. The shoes were tighter than ever, but looking at her beloved groom waiting at the altar made her forget the pain and discomfort, if only momentarily.

"After the wedding ceremony, which seemed interminable because of her aching feet, the bride and her groom went to the reception. There she danced with her new husband, celebrating their union of love. And to her surprise, something delightful happened: the more she danced, the less pain she felt. The now not-so-new shoes were really a perfect fit, and the pain and discomfort she felt when she first put them on soon disappeared."

Scripture Study

- Proverbs 10:12
- 1 Corinthians 13:4-7, 13
- 1 Peter 4:8
- 1 John 4:1-18
- 1 Thessalonians 3:12

Study Questions

- If a young couple came to you for advice, how long would you tell them that it takes for a marriage to "feel comfortable, like an old pair of shoes"?
- Has there been something or someone in your life that you now feel you did not give enough time before ending the process or relationship? Share your experience.
- After joining a new church, how long does it take for the average person to feel comfortable in it? How can a church help newcomers feel welcome?
- Why do some relationships grow deeper with time and others seem to stagnate or not go anywhere? Is there something we can do about this?

My Father's House

One day a celebrated artist exhibited his private collection. This was an exciting event for the entire city, because the artist was recognized throughout the world as an artistic genius. Celebrities and dignitaries attended the grand opening of this once-in-a-lifetime event.

Everyone marveled at the beautiful canvases. They gasped at the power of the portraits. They wept at the emotional symmetry of the landscapes. They stood in awe before the canvases filled with color and form that gave forth the passion as only a true genius can create.

In an obscure corner of the gallery there hung a small and simple painting that depicted a modest house on a field. A white picket fence surrounded the house, and a large oak tree with a swing stood on the front yard. Most people passed it by, not even noticing it, hanging as it was in a far corner away from the major works. A small plaque indicated that the painting was titled, *The House of Wisdom*. Except for a boy named Andrew of about nine years of age, no one had so much as glanced at the painting. But the boy had been staring at the painting for several minutes, an indication that it had made the most profound impression on the young one, and it alone seemed worthy of his attention.

Nearby, the celebrated artist took notice of the boy's interest in the nondescript painting hidden from view of most of the patrons. The famous artist stood for a moment behind the boy, then asked, "Why don't you go look at the other paintings?"

Startled, the small boy stared for a moment before managing to respond, "Because this is the best painting in this place."

"Well," replied the artist, amused, "It isn't a bad painting. But it doesn't compare with any of my other works. This is one of my early works, very unsophisticated."

For several minutes the artist tried to convince Andrew of the merit of his other paintings. He explained how his artistic skill had developed beyond that represented in the small painting in the corner. He pointed out his progression as a painter from simple realism to abstract conceptualizations on canvas. But all that was lost on Andrew. He knew what he liked, and he liked the simple painting of the house with the picket fence.

"Why is the painting called *The House of Wisdom?*" asked Andrew with the candor of a curious innocent.

By this time a crowd had gathered around the artist and the boy. All were curious about the attention given to such a simple painting by the boy and the artist. The great artist felt a little embarrassed to be caught in a debate about art with a small boy. His self-consciousness grew as he noticed the crowd looking at the unsophisticated painting he had tried to keep out of sight by placing it in the corner, away from his more celebrated works.

Clearing his throat and raising his nose, the artist looked down on Andrew and said, "The painting is called *The House of Wisdom* because in the eyes of the wise, there is no house there at all—merely the interplay of humanity's greatest intellectual achievement. The house is a confluence of the basic square and triangle, symbols of the keys to the mastery of mathematics, physics, and chemistry. The swing on the tree symbolizes humanity's dominion over nature."

The crowd applauded the artist's explanation, convinced that the painting was not an awkward product of the artist as a young man, but an ingenious commentary on the nature of things—its subtlety to be appreciated only by those sophisticated enough to understand it. Of course, none dared to admit that they hadn't seen the "deeper meaning" of the painting until the artist explained it.

"And what do you have to say to that?" asked the artist of the small boy.

"I just like it because it looks like my father's house," replied Andrew.

Scripture Study

- Genesis 28:10-19
- 1 Samuel 1:1-28
- 1 Chronicles 22:7-11
- Psalm 27:4-5; 84:10; 122:1-9
- Luke 2:43-49

Study Questions

- Is beauty a thing in itself, or is beauty "in the eyes of the beholder"?
- Can the "innocent" see things that the "wise" and "experienced" cannot? Explain.
- If you were to paint a picture titled *The House of Wisdom*, what would it look like?
- Is it necessary that faith be "uncritical"? Explain.

The Best-Laid Plans

One fateful day the Bentley family heard the worst news that a vacationing family could receive: "The hurricane is coming!" At first they ignored the warning given by a local resident of the seaside town they had chosen for their first vacation in years. The morning was beautiful, there wasn't a cloud in the sky, and only a mild gentle breeze was blowing from the coast. They dared hope that it wasn't true. Some grumpy local resident, resentful of tourist traffic, just wanted to ruin their vacation, they speculated. At the very worst, it must be a bad joke and nothing more.

They went to the beach and enjoyed a fun-filled day. They played in the sand, swam in the ocean (as best they could given the tremendous waves that crashed on shore), and even managed to get in some tanning. By the time they returned to the hotel they had completely forgotten about the hurricane. The family unpacked the car and headed for the hotel lobby. They were eager to shower, change clothes, and hurry out for an afternoon of sightseeing.

As they were crossing the hotel lobby toward the elevators, the family noticed that everyone else seemed to be going in the opposite direction. Crowds of people were streaming from the elevators and heading out the door. Confused, they huddled together to avoid being jostled by the rushing wave of guests that flooded out of an elevator. At that moment they heard the hotel clerk call to them from behind the lobby desk.

"You need to evacuate this building immediately," he yelled over the commotion. "The hurricane is coming!"

Surprised and a bit panicky, the Bentley family rushed to their room, packed their bags, and left in less than fifteen minutes—a record time even for a family practiced in the fine art of rushing out to get to church on time on Sunday mornings! Since they had ample money and time, they decided to go north and finish their vacation there. Several miles later they left the threat of the hurricane behind. Disappointed in their change of plans, they resigned themselves to a vacation of a different sort as they headed north. But once again their plans were thwarted upon hearing that a snowstorm was heading in the direction they had mapped out for themselves.

The Bentleys were a resourceful family. Years of playing board games together and an intentional effort to maintain open communication always paid off during family crises. Dad called a family conference, and in no time at all they were all agreed: They would finish out their vacation, at least what was left of it. Determined to have a good time, they headed west, leaving hurricanes and snowstorms behind.

They headed into the setting sun, glad to leave all their problems behind. The western sun beckoned them with promises of adventures in the unique cultures of the Southwest and of the sunny California coast. Unfortunately, their optimism did not last long. Soon after entering the westernmost landscape, they were greeted by an earthquake that sent them speeding back east in panic.

Overwhelmed by their terrible luck, it took the usually optimistic Bentley family two days and three family conferences to regain their confidence and determination. In the end they all agreed, from the oldest to the youngest Bentley, that they had set out to have a vacation and a vacation they would have! And not only that, but they would enjoy it! Nothing would keep them from their well-deserved and long-awaited family vacation.

After some quick thinking and imaginative rescheduling, the Bentleys found themselves on a tropical island in the beautiful Pacific Ocean. "Paradise at last," cried Mom. And they all agreed . . . that is, until a long dormant volcano on the island decided that this was the week to blow its top! An emergency evacuation took them safely away at the last minute, but not before losing half their luggage to the catastrophic event.

A sympathetic travel agent brought a ray of sunshine to the Bentleys' misguided adventures. Free tickets on a cruise ship bound for Europe offered the promise of salvaging their family vacation. For once the now weary family seemed to have something to cheer about. On the cruise ship they were pampered and entertained. There was plenty to eat and plenty to do. As the family started to relax, the youngest Bentley exclaimed, "We should have done this in the first place!" They all laughed in agreement.

But just as they were about to take a family photo in front of the deck pool, fire broke out in the cruise ship's engine room. Within minutes the Bentleys were bobbing in the ocean on lifeboats as the crew fought the fire. The fire spread quickly, but the crew was able to subdue it before it was able to do serious damage. Only a few crew quarters and passenger rooms were damaged by smoke and water. Unfortunately, one of those rooms belonged to the unlucky and glum Bentley family.

That was the last straw for the usually optimistic and resourceful Bentleys. Hurricane, snowstorm, earthquake, volcano, and now a fire at sea—what else could go wrong? Rather than tempt fate, they decided they had had enough vacationing—it was time to go home. Sadly and dejectedly, they gathered what was left of their possessions and started their long trek home.

Scripture Study

- James 4:13-15
- Acts 16:6-10
- Hebrews 6:3
- Genesis 26:18-22

Study Questions

- Have you ever had a "vacation from hell"? What made it so? Share your experience.
- What is your best response to the question, "Why do bad things happen to good people?"
- Do you believe in fate or providence? Either or both? Explain.
- Some people seem to be able to overcome any obstacle that comes their way; others seem unable to get ahead no matter how hard they try. What do you think it takes to succeed against all odds?

The Best Deal

Once upon a time—a long, long, time ago in fact—there lived a very powerful king who ruled over a kingdom called Malice. This king was extraordinarily rich. His fortune surpassed that of all other kings of his age. Not even King Solomon's fabled wealth compared to the opulence of the king of Malice.

But despite his riches, the king was not a happy person. Although he had all the material things any person could desire, he lacked one thing he could not possess: the love of his people. The people of the kingdom of Malice weren't just indifferent to the king; they loathed him. This was puzzling, because the king was not a bad person or a bad ruler. In fact, he was known far and wide for his benevolent and just rule. His palace was always accessible to his subjects, and the taxes he imposed on them were reasonable.

Despite the fact that a noble and kind king sat on the throne, a lazy and wicked people populated the kingdom of Malice. No one ever visited the king in his palace. No one ever visited the court to seek help with a problem, to ask for intervention, or to suggest a solution to a social condition as was his or her right. And despite the constant complaint about the taxes, no one in Malice actually paid it. The populace had no respect for their king or his court.

The king had tried often to win the respect of his subjects, but nothing seemed to work. When he sent messengers bearing good news throughout the land, they returned beaten and humiliated. When he sent gifts to the governors and princes of his provinces, they were unacknowledged or returned unopened. So desperately vain and bent of spirit were the citizens of Malice that they never appreciated that their king had the power to save them from their self-imposed miseries.

One day the prince, the king's only son, approached his father. Noticing how sad he looked and knowing that the king's only heartache was his obstinate people, he said, "Here, Father, I will go out and conquer the heart of the people for you."

"And how will you do that, my son?" asked the king.

The prince remained silent; he had no reply. He knew that his father had tried everything he could think of to win the heart of his stubborn people, but to no avail. At a loss for ideas, they both sat in silence for the better part of an hour. Then suddenly, the king hit upon an idea he had not thought of before.

"I know!" he exclaimed. "You will go to the people and make them the best deal of their lives."

The king explained his plan to the enthusiastic prince. Immediately they made preparations for the prince's venture among the people of the land of Malice. They ordered that one hundred large wagons be filled with treasures from the king's vast vaults—gold, silver, precious stones, jewelry, and works of art. In addition, there would be bins full of the finest clothing ever seen and two carts filled with the most exotic foodstuffs in the world. When all was ready, the prince set out into the land of Malice, leaving behind the palace with the king anxiously waiting at the gate, praying for his son's success.

On the third day the prince arrived at a large city. He entered the gates and parked his wagons in the town's large public square. He leaped on top of one of the wagons and began to call the people to gather. Soon, almost the entire population was gathered around the square, curious to hear what the stranger had to say.

"Listen, all!" cried the prince. "I have come in the name of my father the king to make you the best deal in the world."

"And what kind of a deal would that be?" cried a heckler from the crowd.

"The king knows we are poor," cried another. "Perhaps he wants to take advantage of us?"

"Yes!" yelled another. "The king is trying to cheat us."

The prince held up his hand for silence. "The deal is very simple," he cried. "All you need to do is to remove your old dusty, worn clothes and give them to me."

"What?" laughed one woman. "And then we're to all stand here naked I suppose!"

The prince waited for the laughter and hooting to die down, then he patiently explained the deal. Anyone who was willing to remove their dirty clothes right there and then would receive in return a fine rich garment. In addition, they would be able to take as much treasure as they could carry in their arms from one of the wagons. Afterward they would be allowed to eat from the delicacies in the food wagons, and they would be able to travel to the king's palace to eat at his table as long as they lived. Moreover, for any who wished, an ample and furnished room would be available for them in the palace to live out the rest of their days.

"The king desires nothing more than to live with his people and to share his wealth with them," explained the prince. "Now, who will be the first to make this deal?"

The prince paused, holding before him an exquisite robe. But the crowd remained silent. No one came forward. Soon a chilly look of suspicion came across the faces of the men and women in the crowd.

The confused prince again explained the deal to the crowd. This time the crowd responded with murmurings, curses, and taunts. Then, two or three in the crowd threw stones at the prince, and the crowd was on the verge of becoming a mob.

"Very well!" cried the Prince, indignant of this treatment. "I will return to my father's palace. The deal is off."

But at that moment something unexpected happened. Hundreds of children let go of their parent's hands and ran toward the prince. There, before all present, the children began to take off their ratty, torn clothes—some merely rags—and laid them at the feet of the prince. Immediately, they were given new clothes—the cleanest, softest, finest, and most luxurious they had ever seen. Soon, standing before the prince in their finery, the children made for a resplendent sight!

The men and women stepped forward, but a look from the prince stopped them in their tracks.

"Will you remove your filthy clothes and put on the king's robes?" he challenged.

But the crowd was frozen in place, torn between their greedy desire for the riches the king offered and their pride and vanity that did not allow them to humble themselves as the children had. They remained frozen in their agonizing dilemma as they watched the prince lead the children toward the king's palace to live forever, to feast at the king's table and enjoy the riches he so desperately wanted to share with all his subjects.

Scripture Study

- Matthew 18:1-4; 19:14
- Isaiah 9:6, 7
- 2 Corinthians 8:9
- John 10:28; 14:1-3
- Revelation 3:18; 20:15

Study Questions

- Do you think that God's forgiveness is complete and comprehensive? Why?
- How easy is it for you to forgive others completely? Is there someone whom you have yet to forgive in some way? If so, how does this affect your Christian faith?
- Some people seem to find it difficult to accept forgiveness. Why?
- As we grow older, does it become easier or more difficult to extend and receive forgiveness? Why?

The Center of God's Will

Doug and Karen are a couple who knew the meaning of contentment. They lived in a lovely home, ample and comfortable. It had a large backyard in which their three children spent countless hours playing. One small patch was set aside for Karen's garden, a welcome pastime and distraction from her job. The house was in a nice neighborhood near a cul-de-sac. On summer evenings Doug and Karen would sit on their front porch sharing memories with their children, sharing hopes about the future, and talking to the occasional neighbor who would drop by to enjoy a glass of lemonade or iced tea in the middle of an evening walk.

But all that ended one day. Though the house was truly home to Doug and Karen, it was not theirs. They rented the home from a man whose daughter was about to be married. Naturally, the daughter wanted to move into the home in which she had grown up—the house that was occupied by Doug and Karen's family. So the family that had enjoyed years of happy living in a home that was just about a perfect fit found themselves having to evacuate and pull up roots within a few weeks.

After weeks of searching for a new place to live, Karen and Doug found a modest two-room apartment closer to the city. It was the only affordable place they could find. Compared to their former neighborhood, it was not very pleasant, but it was better than several other places they had looked.

The first months in that "shoebox"—as one of the children called their sparse apartment—were filled with frustrations and anxiety. Doug often found himself feeling angry, and Karen, despite her best efforts at keeping everyone's spirits up, found herself feeling depressed. She grieved the loss of her lovely garden and of the home they had enjoyed—the only real home they all knew together as family.

There was much about apartment living that contributed to the family's frustration. There was lack of privacy and certainly not enough bathrooms. Lack of storage space made their small living space cluttered. Noise and loud music from the adjacent apartments were a constant source of stress. But worse of all, perhaps, was that the children were not able to play outside. The neighborhood was not safe. Every week brought news of vandalism and stolen cars.

In their quiet moments Doug and Karen would wonder where God was in all this. When they were comfortable in their old home, they thought they felt God's blessings every day. They were grateful in the midst of their contentment. Now God seemed distant. Their prayers for peace of mind seemed to go unanswered.

It so happened that at Doug and Karen's apartment complex there were many other young couples. Several had small children about the ages of their own children. All were of modest income, and as Doug and Karen got to know them, they discovered that they all had problems and struggles. It did not take long for Karen and Doug to realize that the problems of their neighbors were much worse than any they had ever faced. These families had material needs and physical and spiritual problems that made Karen and Doug's situation seem like a minor inconvenience by comparison.

Little by little Doug and Karen regained their sense of gratitude for the life God had granted them: their family, the health of their children, their jobs, and their faith. Soon, they regained their sense of contentment, and with it, the peace of mind they thought they had lost and left behind in their old home. They decided they had not lost it after all; they just forgot to unpack it when they moved into their apartment.

Soon Karen and Doug were spending more time with the young families in their apartment complex. Doug and the children played ball with the kids in the neighborhood. Karen visited with the young mothers and even managed to plant a small flower garden at the entrance of their apartment building. If a neighbor needed help, Doug and Karen were the first to know. If a young couple needed advice, Karen and Doug were the first they'd ask. Neighbors felt free sharing their burdens with this new couple. They seemed to care, always had a kind word, and would listen patiently and compassionately to their neighbors' worries. By year's end Karen and Doug organized a block party. Many neighbors met each other for the first time, despite having lived in the same building for years. And not a few young families started to go to church with Doug and Karen as they openly shared their faith in God.

Doug and Karen lived in that apartment for many years. Though they often dreamed of owning a home like the one they had loved so much, they never moved. And we don't know if it's because they never were able to afford it or if perhaps they decided not to leave. But this we do know: Doug and Karen felt called to their new life in the small apartment in the less-than-idyllic neighborhood. Every life touched, every marriage salvaged, every young life reclaimed from the street, every couple that became a friend, and every soul saved was a confirmation of that. Karen and Doug discovered that the secret of contentment has less to do with where you live and more to do with feeling the certainty of being in the center of God's will.

Scripture Study

- Psalm 37:5; 40:8
- Matthew 4:1; 6:10; 26:42
- Hebrews 10:1-5
- Genesis 12:1-5
- John 4:34; 6:38

Study Questions

- Have you ever experienced a "change in fortune" for the worst? Share your experience.
- Have you ever felt like "getting away from it all" and living a simpler, uncomplicated life? Why or why not?
- Can material wealth be detrimental to the Christian life? Why or why not?
- What is your definition of "contentment"? What would make you content?

Secret Love

Once upon a time, in a field near a pond, there lived a cricket that had the distinction of being the ruling prince of the meadow. He ruled over all insects, large and small, in that self-contained, verdant part of the world.

Every day the cricket would go about his future kingdom clothed in his finest regalia. His yellow-green cape was the envy of the other young courtier crickets. All of the female crickets, of course, were madly in love with him; each one harbored secret dreams of his falling in love with her and making her his princess. But he was oblivious to any of those adoring females of his species, for the love of his life was a humble but beautiful ant that lived in a neighboring meadow.

Every day the cricket ended his excursion at the spot where the two kingdoms bordered and where he knew he would be able to gaze upon the object of his love. There, on the other side of a small rivulet, the beautiful and petite ant gazed back.

The cricket's love, however, was a secret love, for he never confessed his adoration to the ant. Perhaps it was out of timidity, or of fear of being rejected, that he could never bring himself to declare his feelings. Sometimes he wondered if the reason he never told the ant of his love was an imagined public embarrassment if the other crickets found out; or perhaps it was merely the all-too-insecure fear of public opinion on the part of a politico in the making. Whatever the reason, the love that drove him to end his days with the ant's gentle image on his mind was never revealed or spoken.

Ironically, unknown to the cricket prince, the ant who was the focus of his desire loved him in return—with as fervent a love as he had for her. Every day she saw him gazing over the meadow she gazed back, not in curiosity as he often imagined, but with a longing heart. Every time she gazed upon his princely countenance her heart would melt in the passion of her love for him.

But her love, too, remained a secret. She never spoke to the prince; it was not the custom of female ants to declare their love for another first. Besides, as far as she was concerned, the notion that the prince was interested in her was merely wishful thinking on her part.

What could a member of the royal family possibly see in a humble ant from across the meadow? Surely that look he gave her every day was no more than curiosity—a privileged son amused at how the other half lives.

And so two hearts filled with love remained silent hearts, becoming vessels of a secret love never declared. That secret love burned for years in the guarded chambers of their hearts, and with the passing of time that love starved in cocoons unable to sustain it. The gentle confessions that could have set their love free and given it wings were never spoken. Years passed, and both the ant and the prince died waiting for a love so easily within their reach; and with their deaths, a love that might have been died with them.

Scripture Study

- Romans 5:8
- John 3:16; 21:15-17
- Ephesians 5:2
- Galatians 5:13
- 1 John 3:18

Study Questions

- Have you ever loved someone secretly? Did you eventually share how you felt? Why or why not?
- Is it difficult for us to let others know how we feel about them? Why?
- Does love require reciprocation? Why or why not?
- Can you distinguish the qualitative difference between romantic love, fraternal love, familial love, and infatuation? What other kinds of love can you identify?

Index

Topic

Scripture

Printed in Great Britain
by Amazon

53713692R00076